CW01301784

ACKNOWLEDGEMENTS

process of developing a book that makes a unique and timely contribution to current understanding of illicit drug markets, and challenges some of the taken-for-granted assumptions about so-called county lines. I would like to thank Linda for her support, encouragement and insight over the course of the book's development. Finally, a very quick mention for Megan and Daniel.

Carlton Brick

Thanks to my co-authors James Densley and Carlton Brick, as well as my colleagues Ross Deuchar, Chris Holligan, Simon Harding, Dev Maitra, Irene Rafanell, Gareth Rice, Grace Robinson and Mo Rahman. Shout out to my friends: Gary, Moe, Fuzzy, Skippy, Scott, Wullie A., Ross A., Dooltz, Finley, Purdy, Gordy, Wade, Geo, Demps, John, Del, Shearer, Denton (aka Donnie), Steg (aka Chow), Jerry, Scotty, Gav, Adds, Frazer, Ross T., Goffer, Chewy, Michael, Cole, the boys from the footy, the guys from church and all the rest from everywhere else. I would also like to mention my extended family: Jojo, Karnage, Marie and her brothers, Laurie, Andy and Chaz, James and Annie, Mush and his brothers, Aunt Mary and Uncle Jamie, Aunt Annie and Uncle John, Aunt Kit and Uncle Jim, Uncle Peter and Aunt Rosie, Uncle John and Margret, Aunt Christine and Uncle George, and Uncle S. and Aunt J. Thanks also to my in-laws John, Tam, Steph, Gordon, Sheila and John McC's family, as well as wee Ethan.

This book is for the people of Govan, Renfrew and Ferguslie Park, and all the young lives lost in those estates. For: Grant Henderson, Christopher Shand, June and Andy; Andrew Watson, Lee Brown and Frazer Conner; Steve Adams and Frazer McKendrick; Frazer's mate wee Jamie and Don's cousin Davy; and Johnny White, String's mate Sean, Moe's older brother Gorms and Jack from Govan. People read about gang violence, knife crime and drug harms in Glasgow in the newspapers like they are abstract phenomena. I would urge readers to look at these names again and then take a moment to remember that they are not statistics, but people. Their lives matter. A close family friend recently said: "We die twice in life: once in body and the second time in the memory of those whom we know and shared this life with." It is up to us to see that does not happen.

Robert McLean

First and foremost, great thanks go to co-authors James Densley and Robert McLean for the opportunity to be part of the

Acknowledgements

Writing ethnographic research from 4,000 miles away is a challenge at the best of times, more so amid a global pandemic, so my biggest thanks go to my colleagues and co-authors Robert McLean and Carlton Brick for making this book possible, and to our interviewees for graciously sharing their stories with us. Thanks also to colleagues and co-authors past who have taught me so much about gangs, crime and county lines: Scott Decker, Ross Deuchar, David Pyrooz, Simon Harding, Grace Robinson, Michelle Lyttle Storrod, Andrew Whittaker, and others. Thanks to the team at Metro State University and Jillian Peterson at The Violence Project for their patience and support. Finally, special thanks to my friends and family, especially my wife Emily and children Alex and Andrew for making it all worthwhile. I dedicated the last book I wrote with Robert, *Robbery in the Illegal Drugs Trade* (Bristol University Press, 2022), to my dad Andrew, who died in 2020 when we were in the middle of writing it. I would like to dedicate this one to my mum Jan, who has weathered the storm of losing her soulmate with courage, dignity, grace, even humour; she is truly inspiring.

James A. Densley

Thanks be to God for the blessings I have been given. This book is for my amazing wife Nicola (whom I love with all my heart), our children Chloe, Jack, Max, Clair and Faith, and our grandson Jackson. I would like to thank my mum for standing in the face of adversity and overcoming the difficulties in her life. I would like to mention my brothers William, Leonard and Graeme, whom I love dearly. Graeme, you are still my brother and if you ever turn your life around, the door is always open. I would like to mention Hannah, Izzy, Gabriella, Cherie, Kay, Leo, Ciera and Lenny's brothers.

Notes on the Authors

James A. Densley, DPhil (Oxon), is Professor and Department Chair of the School of Law Enforcement and Criminal Justice at Metro State University, US.

Robert McLean, PhD, is Lecturer in the School of Education and Social Sciences at the University of the West of Scotland, UK.

Carlton Brick, PhD, is Lecturer in the School of Education and Social Sciences at the University of the West of Scotland, UK.

Contents

Notes on the Authors   iv
Acknowledgements   v

one	County Lines and the 'Standard Story': An Introduction	1
two	Whose Line Is It Anyway?	20
three	Joining the Line	34
four	Life on the Line	50
five	Crossing the Line	69
six	End of the Line	86
seven	County Lines in a Therapy Culture: A Conclusion	99

Notes   117
References   118
Index   127

JAMES A. DENSLEY, ROBERT MCLEAN
AND CARLTON BRICK

CONTESTING COUNTY LINES

Case Studies in Drug Crime and
Deviant Entrepreneurship

BRISTOL
UNIVERSITY
PRESS

First published in Great Britain in 2023 by

Bristol University Press
University of Bristol
1–9 Old Park Hill
Bristol
BS2 8BB
UK
t: +44 (0)117 374 6645
e: bup-info@bristol.ac.uk

Details of international sales and distribution partners are available at
bristoluniversitypress.co.uk

© Bristol University Press 2023

British Library Cataloguing in Publication Data
A catalogue record for this book is available from the British Library

ISBN 978-1-5292-3206-6 hardcover
ISBN 978-1-5292-3209-7 ePub
ISBN 978-1-5292-3210-3 ePdf

The right of James A. Densley, Robert McLean and Carlton Brick to be identified
as authors of this work has been asserted by them in accordance with the
Copyright, Designs and Patents Act 1988.

All rights reserved: no part of this publication may be reproduced, stored in
a retrieval system or transmitted in any form or by any means, electronic,
mechanical, photocopying, recording or otherwise, without the prior permission
of Bristol University Press.

Every reasonable effort has been made to obtain permission to reproduce copyrighted
material. If, however, anyone knows of an oversight, please contact the publisher.

The statements and opinions contained within this publication are solely those
of the authors and not of the University of Bristol or Bristol University Press.
The University of Bristol and Bristol University Press disclaim responsibility
for any injury to persons or property resulting from any material published in
this publication.

Bristol University Press works to counter discrimination on grounds of gender,
race, disability, age and sexuality.

Cover design: Bristol University Press
Front cover image: Getty/David Wall
Bristol University Press uses environmentally responsible
print partners.
Printed and bound in Great Britain by CPI Group (UK) Ltd,
Croydon, CR0 4YY

ONE

County Lines and the 'Standard Story': An Introduction

Introduction

"I know it when I see it" – these are the famous words US Supreme Court Justice Potter Stewart used to define hard-core pornography in *Jacobellis v. Ohio* (378 U.S. 184, 1964). The phrase was Potter's attempt to categorize an observable fact or event – in this case, pornography – when that category was subjective or lacked clearly defined parameters.

This book asks whether 'I know it when I see it' has become a problem in the context of county lines drug dealing. No two county lines are perfectly alike, but they are all defined in roughly the same terms that privilege certain concepts, borrowed from psychology and public health, like 'child exploitation' and 'vulnerability'. There is now a 'standard story' (Pfaff, 2017) about the causes of county lines and the profiles and motivations of their protagonists and antagonists that has become a way of seeing (for a discussion, see Spicer, 2019). However, as Pfaff (2017) demonstrates in the context of mass incarceration, standard stories not only tend to limit knowing something when you see it, but also might prevent us from seeing it at all. The standard story is not 'wrong' per se; rather, it captures very legitimate concerns. The problem is that it emphasizes those concerns at the expense of other things, things that potentially matter more when it comes to problem solving.

The 'county lines' concept first appears in a National Crime Agency (NCA) intelligence assessment published in 2015, based on 2014 'returns from police forces following the circulation of a national intelligence requirement ... information from the Home Office Gang and Youth Violence front line team, force problem profiles, subject matter experts and academic literature' (NCA, 2015: 2). Readers of that original 'threat' assessment will observe that discussion of the 'national issue' of county lines, which 'almost always involves exploitation of vulnerable persons' and the 'essential feature' of 'mobile phone lines', has hardly changed at all in years since (NCA, 2015: 1). Such consistency is rare in social science: either the police forces, the Home Office and 'subject matter experts' defined this problem perfectly out of the gate, or the police forces, the Home Office and 'subject matter experts' created a self-fulfilling prophecy. There is a chance that the research confirming county lines that followed did so because it overlooked the diversity of county lines activity as evidence of country lines at all.[1]

Take, for example, the allegedly integral role of 'gangs' in county lines. County lines networks are commonly described as urban drug dealers who advertise and sell to customers in more rural areas via dedicated phone lines (Coliandris, 2015; Windle and Briggs, 2015a; Storrod and Densley, 2017; Harding, 2020; McLean et al, 2020). However, Andell and Pitts (2018: 5, emphasis added) define county lines as 'an embedded, national, drug distribution system, which has both fostered and become reliant upon local, stratified, third generation *street gangs*'. The NCA's (2015: 2) original report equates 'urban street gangs' with 'organised crime groups', 'dangerous dealer networks', 'transient drug dealers' and, simply, 'group'. This all-encompassing terminology meant that the drug-dealing practices of practically any entity fell under the rubric of county lines.

The 'standard story' of county lines actors is that they are organized drug dealers who exploit children and vulnerable adults (Havard et al, 2021; Moyle, 2019; Robinson et al, 2019;

Windle et al, 2020; Brewster et al, 2021). They operate in big cities (or saturated markets, see Windle and Briggs, 2015b; Hales and Hobbs, 2010) and expand their activity into rural and coastal towns (untapped, growing markets) by pushing out local dealers and targeting unmet demand (Andell, 2019; Coomber and Moyle, 2018). They are attracted to remote areas by the combination of the potential customer base and low resistance from local dealers who lack the same criminal capacity and capability (NCA, 2015, 2017, 2019). They then expand their workforce by recruiting local runners to deliver drugs and money (Jaensch and South, 2018). There is ample evidence to support each of these claims, but the question is: are they true of every county line all the time?

Drug supply is the most prevalent form of organized crime in Britain and can be a financial boon for the offenders involved (Black, 2020). It also costs taxpayers billions each year in social and economic harm (Stevens, 2011). Before county lines, major cities served as national supply 'hubs' for illegal drugs trafficked from overseas (Pearson et al, 2001). Organized criminals shipped in bulk to regional wholesalers then drugs would filter into local retail markets through transactions undertaken by local low-level retailers (Matrix Knowledge Group, 2007) and 'user-dealers' resident in the area (Coomber, 2006). Global capitalism and technologies like smartphones and social media changed these criminal and routine activities (Pitts, 2008; Densley et al, 2018; Deuchar et al, 2021), creating a 'networked territoriality' (Clark et al, 2021) that enables county lines networks to blur boundaries both between urban and rural, and between national (wholesale) and local (retail), dealing. Actors in 'hub' cities now commute to remote 'host' sites not only to wholesale product, but also to retail it there on the streets (Coomber and Moyle, 2018; Windle and Briggs, 2015a).

County lines are implicated in the economic expansion of criminal gangs (Whittaker et al, 2020b) and in spreading knife crime, gun crime and other forms of serious violence to small towns unaccustomed to 'big city' problems (HMG,

2018). A public policy priority has been to protect vulnerable people who are forced to sell drugs on behalf of gangs, or who unwillingly have their homes used by gangs for their operations – known as 'cuckooing' (Coomber and Moyle, 2018 Spicer et al, 2020). In fact, county lines are viewed in practitioner circles almost exclusively through the lens of child criminal exploitation and 'vulnerability' (Coliandris, 2015), human trafficking and modern slavery (Secretary of State for the Home Department, 2019). However, owing to the racialized construction of UK 'gangs' (see Hallsworth and Young, 2008; Smithson et al, 2012; Williams, 2015; Gunter, 2017) and a knowledge bias towards county lines operating out of English 'hub' cities in general, in particular, London (Densley et al, 2020), public perception of county lines may not be entirely representative of the diversity of county lines activity (see Harding, 2020). There is a risk that law enforcement agencies are policing the *mythology* of county lines, not its *reality* (Spicer, 2019, 2021b, 2021c).

For example, recent studies have found that *street* gangs are not nearly as *street* as the name implies (McLean et al, 2019). Street orientation is less a fixed attribute and more a variable one, contingent on the evolution and activity of the gang (Densley, 2013), as well as its cultural adaptation to technology and other drug market developments (Whittaker et al, 2020a). Likewise, research has discovered that *child* exploitation in county lines is not as clear-cut as it sounds. First, the youthfulness of county lines gangs may be exaggerated. While county lines have been linked to *vulnerable* children going missing from school, home or care, and/or being found in areas miles from home (Sturrock and Holmes, 2015; Moyle, 2019), many of the people arrested in county lines operations are adults with dubious vulnerability claims (NCA, 2015, 2017, 2019).

Second, while it is true that some young people in county lines do not realize their own exploitation (Densley, 2012b; The Children's Society, 2019) and even exploit others to make themselves feel better about their own exploited status

(Robinson et al, 2019), there is evidence to suggest that people enter into county lines of their own volition and their peer networks are not nearly as coercive as the standard story suggests (Hesketh, 2019; Harding, 2020; McLean et al, 2020; Bonning and Cleaver, 2021). Framing the issue of county lines more around the 'profit maximization' of calculating criminals and less around endemic social and structural problems simply absolves powerful actors of any responsibility for the expansion of the illegal drugs trade or the collateral consequences of their attempts to police it (Spicer, 2019, 2021a). There is some irony to the fact that the racialized and marginalized youth who the state once criminalized for participation in the illegal economy, now are recast as vulnerable victims in need of state protection – not least because state or structural exclusions are partly to blame for people's vulnerability and victimization in the first place.

For some youth, joining gangs and selling drugs is merely an adaptation to rising inequality and sociocultural exclusion in Britain after Brexit and a decade of austerity cuts to public expenditure (Densley and Stevens, 2015; Irwin-Rogers, 2019; Marsh, 2019; Deuchar et al, 2021). For marginalized youth in Merseyside, for example, 'grafting' by drug dealing was merely a substitute for the lack of meaningful work in the local economy (Hesketh, 2019). Hesketh (2019) memorably documents a pattern of 'deviant entrepreneurship', whereby youth apply desirable entrepreneurial knowledge and business enterprise skills illegally to make ends meet (see also Densley, 2013; Hesketh and Robinson, 2019). The case studies in this book speak directly to this concept, hence its use in our subtitle.

Correspondingly, the alleged *intelligent design* of county lines feels overstated. The standard story implies that the mobile phone is king and county lines drug dealers are sophisticated cybercriminals (for a discussion, see Moyle et al, 2019), but in reality, anyone can send a message on Snapchat or WhatsApp, and in the age of social media, criminal offending that transpires both in person and online at the same time is common (Storrod and Densley, 2017; Roks et al, 2021). The standard story further suggests that drug-dealing gangs conduct a market and competitive analysis of target areas before moving in on them, strategically occupying spaces where demand for drugs is high, supply is low and formal and informal social controls are lacking (Andell, 2019). Yet, correlation is not causation – the last part of this sentence may be true even if the first part is not.

For example, in the US in the 1990s, there was a comparable narrative about gangs spreading nationwide to expand and export their drug-trafficking operations. Maxson (1998) famously examined this claim and found that the most common migration pattern for gang members was a move for social reasons to improve their quality of life and get closer to family and friends. Law enforcement presumed drug sales were a greater motivation for gang migration than they actually were, and individual migration preceded the emergence of gangs in only 5 per cent of the cities surveyed.

Relatedly, the perceived novelty of county lines seems inflated. What the English call 'county lines' is, to some extent, what the Scottish call 'good old-fashioned drug dealing', owing to the country's history, geography, connectivity and population distribution (Holligan et al, 2020). Furthermore, in both countries, 'commercial dealers' who sell drugs for financial gain have long utilized a low-paid workforce to courier, store and sell drugs on their behalf (May and Hough, 2004; Coomber, 2006; Pitts, 2008). As early as 2012, Densley (2014: 533) warned about senior gang members employing young people to work their 'drugs line' by sending them out 'on assignment' outside of London to explore 'new markets'. Reminiscent of Levitt and Venkatesh's (2000) study of a 'drug-selling gang' in Chicago and the income and risk disparities they found between senior gang members and their foot soldiers, Densley (2012b) likened the gang to a 'pyramid scheme', whereby gang 'elders' at the top exploited their 'downline' of 'younger' drug runners and sellers at the bottom to maximize profits and avoid police attention.

Drug distribution networks change over time and place in line with the socio-economic impacts of and on culture and agency (Dorn et al, 1992; Seddon, 2006), and several models of drug distribution can run concurrently owing to supply-and-demand pressures. With this in mind, this book is what drug dealers might call a 're-up' to our 2020 short, *County Lines: Criminal Networks and Evolving Drug Markets in Britain* (McLean et al, 2020). That book offered a general introduction to the county lines phenomenon, together with insights from offenders, victims and practitioners in Merseyside (England) and Glasgow (Scotland). To highlight some of the finer points of county lines and contest some of the 'standard story' we ourselves helped construct, the current study dives deeper into the lived experience of county lines and offers two empirical case studies from the Scottish research site.

Drawing on a series of qualitative interviews and ethnographic observations, this book offers 'thick descriptions' (Geertz, 1973) of: why and how county lines start and end; the structure and operation of county lines; the recruitment and retention processes in county lines, including coercion and exploitation; the motivations of the actors involved; the social and emotional bonds they share; and the (unintended) consequences of their words and deeds. At times, our two county lines case studies deviate from the standard story of county lines, thus challenging popular misconceptions about drug-dealing networks and debunking a few myths that colour decision making about how best to tackle them.

Our cases are presented chronologically and in an accessible style consistent with 'narrative criminology' (Presser and Sandberg, 2015). On occasion, we recreate moments in time, including dialogue between our interviewees that is not strictly verbatim, but rather faithfully reconstructed from our interview transcripts. We do this to contextualize our findings and breathe life into our central 'characters', for they are, after all, real human beings. We hope this device helps readers – students and scholars in criminology, sociology and public health, as well as policy makers and practitioners in criminal justice, education, social care and healthcare – to better understand county lines and the people and places involved in them.

Data sources and methods

As discussed, this short book is shaped by the voices of actors 'situated' within Scotland's illegal drugs market (McLean et al, 2018), not those who seek to influence the market externally, such as law enforcement agencies. Informed by 'narrative criminology' theory and in acknowledgement of the transformative power of personal stories (Presser and Sandberg, 2015), this book takes readers deep inside two county lines drug-dealing networks. It is built on the foundation of nearly a decade of ethnographic fieldwork in Glasgow and West Scotland, as well as qualitative interviews with hundreds of men and women who were at one time embedded in gangs and group offending (for a discussion of 'embeddedness', see Decker et al, 2022), and/or activity defined by Police Scotland as 'organized crime' (see Densley et al, 2019; McLean, 2019; McLean and Densley, 2020, 2022).

For this book, a purposive sample of current and ex-offenders sat for a series of in-depth interviews focused specifically on their experience with county lines. This hard-to-reach population snowballed out from the participants and personal contacts of our prior research studies, shedding light on the lives of 20 people. Interviews were mostly done one on one and face-to-face in people's homes or in coffee shops; however, the global pandemic in 2020 and 2021 meant that some interviews reverted to FaceTime and WhatsApp, and some clarifying questions were answered via WhatsApp voice notes and messages. The average interview was an hour long, with a range of 30 minutes to five hours, and most interviewees sat for at least two interviews, sometimes many more.

Interviews were conducted during 2020–21 and reflect upon an important time in the 'glocal' drugs economy (Hobbs, 1998) when the increased prevalence of cheaper, stronger drugs caused drug deaths in Scotland to spike. The price of illicit drugs was falling while purity was improving, and the local drugs trade, initially assumed to have been led by demand, was increasingly described in policy and practice circles as becoming supply-led, incorporating some franchised 'partners' and their newly recruited 'runners' (Andell, 2019).

The University of the West of Scotland granted ethical approval for the study. Participation was voluntary and predicated on the active and informed consent of all research participants. Standard ethical principles were followed regarding informed consent, right to withdrawal and data protection. Interviews were either digitally recorded and selectively transcribed, or captured directly via voice notes. The data were coded and analysed thematically, and verbatim quotes (with the distinctive Glaswegian slang and patois fully preserved) are used throughout the book to illustrate these themes and recreate dialogue and 'scenes' from the past that help contextualize our findings. Pseudonyms are used to preserve the confidentiality of the respondents, and some details have been spliced and edited for the same reason.

The 'hub' site: Glasgow

As discussed, county lines involve criminal groups establishing a drug distribution network between an urban 'hub' and a remote 'county' location into which drugs are supplied. In this book, our hub city is Glasgow – the drug supply emanates from there.

Glasgow is the largest city in Scotland but not its capital, and for decades, it was regarded as a redundant, post-industrial 'city of gangs', divided by violent sectarianism and fuelled by drugs and alcohol (Deuchar, 2009; Davies, 2013; Fraser, 2015). Poverty and inequality are entrenched, with over a fifth of the city's children living in unemployed households; in some communities, over 50 per cent of youth live below the poverty line (Glasgow Indicators Project, 2015). So too is organized crime, which is omnipresent in Glasgow, hidden in plain view (Fraser et al, 2018; McLean and Densley, 2020).

The Scottish Index of Multiple Deprivation has consistently shown that a disproportionate number of the country's most deprived communities are located in and around Glasgow (Scottish Government, 2020). Problematic drug use is highest in these areas of deprivation. In the 1980s and 1990s, opiates such as heroin and methadone, and non-prescribed benzodiazepines such as etizolam ('street Valium'), which high-risk opioid users misuse either to increase the effects of heroin or methadone or treat withdrawal symptoms and undiagnosed psychiatric disorders, became a dangerous adaptation to poverty in the city. A significant increase in problem drug users in Glasgow peaked about 20 years ago, but there is now an ageing 'Trainspotting' generation of drug addicts (Daly, 2017), mainly men, who have been abusing opiates for decades (Casey et al, 2009). Scotland has the highest recorded drug death rate in Europe (Walsh et al, 2017) and its 'levels of problematic drug use ... and drugs crime are among the highest in the world' (McCarron, 2014: 17).

The 'county' sites: A-Town and B-Town

Geographically speaking, Scotland is not much smaller than England, with which it shares a 60-mile land border; however, England's population of 55 million is over 10 times greater than Scotland's 5 million. The vast majority of Scots live in and around the country's Central Belt, which includes Greater Glasgow, home to nearly 1 million people, and the capital city of Edinburgh, with about 500,000 occupants. Aberdeen and Dundee are the only other settlements in the country with more than 100,000 residents. The rest of Scotland is punctuated by small towns and villages and remote rural communities, each sustained by agriculture and fishing, forestry, and tourism.

Many of these places fell on hard times when deep coal mining and other traditional (heavy) industries collapsed in the 1980s, and they continue to lose young, skilled professionals to the big cities.

Our first provincial site is sparsely populated but covers a large geographical area, including several small, working-class towns and villages. Most of the action in this book takes place in the largest town, which we call '**A-Town**', and two remote villages, which we call 'North Village' and 'South Village'. Graduation rates are low and unemployment rates are high here. Those who have been able to relocate have largely done so. The people left behind live in four-in-a-block cottage houses owned either by the state or by absentee landlords, with two side doors at either end for the upstairs and downstairs homes, or a front door and side door at either end. Occupants have little work and little to do, and they have turned to drugs and alcohol to treat their pain and distract them from the daily grind.

Our second provincial site is similarly a small town, which we call '**B-Town**', surrounded by one large 'Village A' and three small villages. Much like the first site, the area was originally built for heavy industry or local farming expanse, and its population is ageing and in decline. Unlike the first research site, however, a few young professional commuters to the nearest large city live in small newbuild housing estates on the outskirts of the local villages. Overall, houses in the area are mainly four-in-a-block cottages or terrace properties, with front and back doors and private gardens.

Both sites are rural and remote and meet the criteria for county lines. People do not make and manufacture drugs in A-Town and B-Town; rather, drugs end up there because A-Town and B-Town are target markets.

The interviewees in A-Town

Bob is a reformed offender who has desisted from a life of crime. As a teenager, whenever adults were around, Bob was quiet, well mannered and well behaved. He was the one kid on the block that all the local mothers wanted their sons to be like. However, when the adults were away, Bob liked to play, and today he is known as a street fighter who if beaten with a fist, comes back with a knife, and if beaten with a knife, comes back with a gun.

Bob's reputation as a 'dangerous hardman' precedes him, but like most reputations, Bob's is inflated. There is a lot of mythmaking in gangs and on the streets (Felson, 2006), meaning that a fight with another local hardman would be spun a yarn and we would suddenly hear Bob credited with defeating two guys singlehandedly. With further embellishment, it would be five guys armed to the teeth that Bob beat with a single punch. Stories have a habit of defining how others see you, and this was certainly the case with Bob. Around us, however, he was a consummate gentleman.

Bob had little to do with drug distribution in his youth, but as a young adult, he made a conscious decision to broker a deal between two independent criminal networks involved in robbery and drug distribution, thus creating a more cohesive organized crime grouping. Bob looked after the group's drug-dealing enterprise. Any money that needed cleaning also moved through Bob.

Billy is Bob's younger brother, and like Bob, he's an enthusiastic weightlifter. Billy was a good boxer in his youth and played for the junior team of a major professional association football club until a stint in one of Scotland's young offenders' institutions for gang fighting brought an abrupt end to his career. When incarcerated, "something changed inside", and Billy says he was "not the same person" after he was released. He became more withdrawn and paranoid that people would always be after him, seeking revenge for crimes past, and so he never left the house without a knife. He also became more aggressive and prone to violent outbursts. Facilitated by the criminal contacts Billy made inside prison, he became a persistent offender involved in drug supply, professional car theft and firearms distribution for nearly two decades. Now in his late 30s, Billy has finally ceased offending and works as a mentor for young people criminally embedded in gangs and suffering from addictions.

Bob and **Grease** are related through reordered family structures. Grease is well acquainted with street life and well networked with known criminals in Glasgow and A-Town. He is an open-book: chatty by nature, with a reputation for wheeling and dealing on the periphery of gangs, and group offending. He has wrestled with drug addiction since he was a teenager, and he occasionally engaged in theft, robbery, burglary and petty drug dealing to feed his habit. Grease also has a short fuse and a history of getting into fights, for which he has served a series of minor prison sentences.

Bob and Billy were once independent drug dealers loosely affiliated with different organized crime groups in Glasgow. By joining forces, the two of them graduated to the lucrative wholesale supply of cocaine, amphetamines and cannabis. Bob was the money man and shared strategic responsibility for the group with his long-time friend **Gary**, who handled cannabis production and sales, while Billy oversaw cocaine distribution. After Grease relocated to A-Town to live with his girlfriend, this burgeoning organized crime syndicate got the idea and opportunity to expand operations outside of Glasgow, following a county lines business model. Sourced directly from Glasgow, Grease was tasked with selling cocaine, Valium and cannabis to A-Town and the surrounding villages, though as we write about later, Bob had reservations about giving Grease so much responsibility.

Billy oversaw the movement of goods, money and people from the Glasgow conurbation to A-Town. Grease was the point man in A-Town and was told to set up operations and recruit local youth to deal drugs in the community. He was given very little support from the group in Glasgow beyond a steady supply of illegal drugs. **Mary**, Grease's fiancée and the mother of his children, met Grease at work (a zero-hours contract at a retail outlet) when she was a university student in Glasgow, and the two of them bonded over recreational drug use. Mary is originally from A-Town and she is the reason Grease moved there.

Mary's younger brother **Jack** shared a flat with his older sister for a few years while he too attended university in Glasgow. This is how he met Grease and how he first developed a drug habit. Owing to the "bright lights of the city" and his party lifestyle, Jack never finished his degree. He moved back home to A-Town, and during a period of separation from Grease, Mary and her children joined him. Mary and Grease eventually reconciled, and the whole family lived under one roof until Mary, Grease and the children got their own place to live nearby. Jack is now a single occupant in a three-bedroom family home, though his friend **Davey** crashes there from time to time. Davey was a local takeaway driver whom Grease recruited to the group to work as a courier.

Allan is good friends with Jack, though a few years younger than him. After his father died of a drug overdose, Allan moved in with his widowed mother in A-Town but sometimes crashes at his uncle's house in North Village. Like his late father, Allan has a drug problem and a reputation locally for being a troublemaker when intoxicated. He is unemployed and has never worked a full-time job in his life, only a series of part-time or cash-in-hand jobs in between education and training courses. It was Grease who brought Allan into the fold, and at the time of writing, Allan is serving a custodial sentence for his role in county lines.

Robert is Grease's younger distant cousin. Robert initially moved from Glasgow to A-Town after Grease had invited him to stay with his family at Jack's house. Once in A-Town, Robert started working for Grease selling drugs and dating **Stacy**, whose mum's pad in South Village became the gang's holding house and centre of operations. Stacy's second cousin **Adam** also helped the group sell drugs from time to time. Robert and Stacy are out of the drugs game now, and Robert works full-time for Stacy's uncle, a local small business owner.

At six feet tall and weighing in at 280 pounds (20 stone), **Del** is called 'Big Del' for a reason. Del has an equally big personality. Like Billy and Grease, Del has been in plenty of fights in his life, including some pretty spectacular ones. He cleaned up his act after he got married in his early 20s, but when his marriage broke down a few years later, Del got back at it, cycling in and out of relationships, and in and out of crime, especially drug dealing. It was Del's idea to give Grease a shot at drug dealing in A-Town. Del served as muscle for the gang back in Glasgow and protected Billy. At the time of writing, he is awaiting sentencing for drug offences.

They say never judge a book by its cover. **Rav** is softly spoken and slenderly built, and he does not immediately strike you as someone capable of great physical violence. However, Rav was muscle for the gang in Glasgow. Rav has stood before the courts in Scotland no less than 20 times charged with such crimes as theft, malicious acts, fraud, drunk and disorderly, anti-social behaviour, car-related offences, robbery, assault, grievous bodily harm, weapons offences, possession of a firearm, and attempted murder. He has served several community payback orders and stints in prison for his actions, and he has spent his entire life battling drug and gambling addictions. At the time of writing, he is back in prison and was recently diagnosed with post-traumatic stress disorder, which stems from his abusive childhood and the time he spent as a youth living on the streets and in homeless shelters.

Finally, **Paddy** is the driver and occasional muscle for the gang in Glasgow. He is small and heavyset, and has always excelled in physical sports, such as rugby, football, judo and wrestling. Paddy stayed largely on the periphery of crime in his youth but was brought into the fold of the drug-dealing network through friendship ties with Bob, Billy and Rav. Following a criminal conviction, Paddy's long-term girlfriend and mother of his children threatened to leave, and that was enough for Paddy to cut ties. He is no longer involved in offending.

This book focuses largely on the county line headed by Grease and events in and around A-Town, but it was Bob,

Billy and others who pulled the strings back in Glasgow. While each actor had a role to play in the business, responsibilities often overlapped and group members frequently challenged one another, occasionally fighting and falling out. No one was ever anointed the group's 'leader', and the roles, responsibilities and rules of the group were informally governed based on years of shared experience and friendship, as well as a generalized 'common knowledge' about everyone's strengths and weaknesses. In other words, this was an 'informal-diffuse' group, even if it may appear 'rational-formal' to outsiders owing to its business orientation (Decker et al, 2022).

The interviewees in B-Town

Amy is the oldest of nine children. Now in her mid-40s, she heads a sizeable and relatively powerful kinship-based 'rational-formal' organized crime group. Amy oversees the strategic planning of this crime family, though much of the daily tactical operations are the remit of her younger brother **Echo**. Amy takes pride in her appearance, and while stern in her words, she speaks with a soft voice. At times, it can be difficult to imagine her leading a criminal enterprise that specializes in lucrative wholesale drug distribution. Amy's initial route into drug dealing was facilitated by her uncle, who sought to aid the family's hardships following the breakdown of the initial family unit. Thereafter, Amy gradually built several connections with powerful organized criminals, and these connections aided the progression of the outfit to the level they currently occupy.

Events in this book start about a decade ago, when, fleeing domestic abuse from **John**, a big-time heroin dealer, Amy relocated from Glasgow to B-Town in the east of Scotland and her brother Echo followed her. "It seemed a good idea at the time", Echo explained. Echo is a large and eccentric man, who is loud and brash. Echo was always close with Amy and has been involved in crime, including the local street gangs in Glasgow, since he was a boy. He was incarcerated for the first time in his late teens, and he has served a series of short prison sentences over the years for various offences, including violent crime, drugs and illegal driving. For a while, Echo lived in the same rented property as Amy and her children, but he later moved to Village A nearby.

Once in B-Town, Amy and Echo started selling drugs sourced from Glasgow directly to local retail dealers. The drugs were initially couriered into B-Town by Amy and Echo's younger brother **Paul**. Paul is about two years younger than Amy and one year younger than Echo, and because they are so close in age, the three of them share a close bond. Like Echo, Paul was involved in youth gangs and juvenile delinquency, but unlike Echo, Paul has struggled with polydrug use. Paul officially lives in Glasgow but lives a nomadic life, and whenever he's moving drugs east or money back west, he frequents some female friends in the local area villages.

James is Echo's childhood friend from Glasgow, who even dated his sister Amy on and off. James was only ever peripherally involved in crime, but his friendship with Echo got him into a lot of fights. **Gordon** is also Echo's friend. He is originally from B-Town but routinely travels back and forth to Glasgow to transport drugs and money with Echo or on his behalf. Gordon is much younger than the rest of the group, and it was through Echo that he fell deeper and deeper into a life of crime, becoming dependent on the money he earned from drug dealing to support his long-term girlfriend and her young child. At the time of writing, Gordon is in prison.

Peter is local to B-Town, where Amy's county line runs, and has extensive kinship networks throughout the region. He is also a long-time heroin addict who reluctantly works for Echo in exchange for money, drugs and debt relief. Finally, **Susanna** is Peter's long-term partner, and while they both have their own homes, Susanna lives primarily at Peter's house. Susanna was born in the area and has known Peter since school, but they only started dating in adulthood when they both became addicted to heroin. Susanna has tried on many occasions to 'become clean', and when she does, she usually moves back into the home she inherited from her mother, who died several years ago. However, the home is severely dilapidated, and Susanna is now looking to sell it to a local buyer or the local redevelopment authority. Susanna and Peter are in their late 30s and have two children together, but owing to their drug addiction, they have lost visitation rights and the children now live with Peter's parents.

Concluding remarks

The purpose of this book is to explore the nuances of county lines drugs networks through two case studies anchored in the lived experiences and spoken narratives of several active participants in Scotland's illegal drugs trade. The chapter opened by reviewing the 'standard story' and existing literature on county lines, drawing attention to not only the inherent harms caused by the growth of the illicit drugs trade in the UK, but also the gaps in our knowledge about how county lines really work. County lines are a diverse drug supply model within an evolving criminal landscape, but they are often narrowly portrayed, and findings from a small number of government reports and academic research studies, including our own, have become profound truths among policy makers, practitioners and the public. Yet, the standard story might conceal as much as it reveals, and the risk is that people do not know county lines when they see them.

This chapter has discussed the data we hope will add greater breadth and depth to the knowledge base around county lines. Having now introduced the actors in this study, we proceed to our findings. In Chapter 2, we examine the personal, non-criminal origins of county lines in A-Town and B-Town. While the capacity for gangs to move product, people and pound notes back and forth between Glasgow and these rural communities always existed, we learn that two unrelated domestic issues are what created the opportunity and incentive for our interviewees to do so. The findings thus challenge some of the standard story about the strategic origins of county lines drugs networks.

Chapter 3 explores selection into county lines, including some of the subtler forms of coercion and exploitation that career criminals use to expand their workforce and influence in the marketplace. The findings here hint at the human agency that complicates the standard story about passive vulnerability in county lines recruitment. While gender regulates a hierarchical difference in traditional male and female roles, moreover, our case studies demonstrate that women occupy a wide range of roles within the county lines economy, including positions of power. This challenges the prevailing opinion about women as subordinate victims or passive participants.

Chapter 4 walks readers through the first few days of drug sales in A-Town, emphasizing the tools, techniques and tactics our interviewees used to ship, store and sell drugs in the area. The extent to which our interviewees embrace or reject mobile phones and 'ring and bring' delivery dealing is discussed. The chapter also explores the dynamics of debt collection and conflict management in B-Town, and precisely why violence can be bad for business. These findings help flesh out the standard story of county lines by illuminating some of the dark corners of the practice and decision-making processes that are usually shrouded in secrecy.

Playing on the immortal words of Ernest Hemingway, Chapter 5 demonstrates how county lines can go bankrupt *gradually* and then *suddenly*. This chapter highlights how personal pride and greed undermine group cohesiveness, and how lies and mistrust ultimately lead to the downfall of the criminal enterprise. This theme continues through Chapter 6, which documents in vivid detail the problem of violence in county lines and the events leading up to the end of the line in A-Town.

Finally, Chapter 7 summarizes our key findings. We conclude with a critical assessment of the county lines standard story, arguing that a medicalized view of the world and a well-meaning but narrow focus on vulnerability and victimhood has contributed to a form of concept creep that may be deleterious to efforts to prevent and prosecute county lines.

TWO

Whose Line Is It Anyway?

Introduction

The 'standard story' on county lines begins with cold and calculating criminals shipping off some poor exploited teenager to the farthest corners of the country to live in filth on the floor of a crack den, sustained by nothing more than a mobile phone and a backpack full of drugs. While this most certainly happens, and it is abhorrent when it does, our county lines case studies start very differently. Here, crime opportunities come second to family commitments as explanations for gang proliferation and gang member migration.

Do for love

Our first case study starts with an adult, Grease, saying his goodbyes to family and friends, standing next to his car, which is "packed out" with bedding, children's toys, furniture and the other essentials for family life. Grease is moving out to try and reconcile with his estranged partner Mary and their children. Mary left Grease a few months prior and moved from Glasgow to A-Town to be closer to her brother, who lives there too, her mother and father, who live in a nearby village, and several aunts, uncles and cousins. Mary was now settled in A-Town, happy even, so this was Grease's desperate final attempt to make things right and make their relationship work. He was moving to the "outback" in the "middle of nowhere" for love – for Mary.

Never one to let a good opportunity go to waste, Grease's family and friends, many of whom were deeply embedded in Glasgow's criminal underworld, had an ulterior motive for Grease's relocation.

"Grease mate, you know what you're going to do once up there right?", Billy asked.

"Aye mate, I've got it sorted. No need to worry about it", replied Grease.

Billy had heard words to this effect many times before from Grease. Billy and Grease were like brothers, but Grease always had a habit of "fucking shit up". Even more so when the task at hand was presumed to be "unfuckable".

Almost like he had read Billy's mind, Bob chimed in, his voice stern: "Just don't fuck it up. Hear me?" Bob was not the gang's leader per se, but he was the most feared group member, so when he talked, others listened.

"I won't mate", said Grease.

"All right then, bring it in." Bob gave Grease a big bearhug.

After a round of hugs, elaborate handshakes and fist bumps, Grease was finally on his way. He waved out of the window until his car disappeared into the distance, and when it did, Bob was left to cope with the sinking feeling that this was a bad idea. He told us: "How was Grease, of all people, going to manage to run any sort of [drugs] operation when he was still going to his mum's house every other week to get his clothes washed, d'you know what I mean?". Grease was hardly self-sufficient or a self-starter.

A few months prior, the group had coalesced around the illegal drugs trade during a meeting to discuss "business opportunities". Before that fateful meeting, the lads were friendly with each another, but they either worked alone or for one of two independent organized crime groups in the area. This was partially due to a five-year age gap between the youngest and oldest members of the group, and different social networks growing up. Still, kinship and mutual trust and respect were key to the creation of this new hybrid group. They had shared in good times and bad and had lost some loved ones to the streets along the way. Drawing on shared experience and 'criminal capital' (McCarthy and Hagan, 1995, 2001), the lads decided that they were stronger united than divided, being better positioned to challenge or withstand challenges from some of the other criminal gangs in the area.

Bob agreed to oversee the group, in part, because he was older and had ties to local business owners and other contacts who could help the group clean their money and invest it in legitimate ventures. Gary was responsible for cannabis production and Billy took charge of the cocaine side of the business. The group agreed that if anyone was ever caught and incarcerated, then their cut of money would not stop. This empowered the group to take more risks. Yet, one risk that Bob and Billy were reluctant to take was bringing Grease into the fold.

Bob and Billy felt that Grease had little to offer the group. While he was well-liked among his peers, Grease was also a bit of a liability in their eyes because his drug binges could go on for weeks and sometimes months. During these times, Grease was "fun to be around" interviewees said, but his behaviour was erratic and the mood swings were hard to take. Grease was "emotionally unstable" and he was also known to leverage his relationship with Bob and Billy and their reputations as "go-aheads" for violence to fling his weight about. To paraphrase the immortal words of Captain Tom 'Stinger' Jordan from the 1986 movie *Top Gun*, Grease's ego would write cheques his body could not cash, and this resulted in Bob and Billy being drawn into needless confrontations with others who had taken issue with something Grease had said or done.

However, when Grease announced to the group that he was moving to A-Town to get Mary back, Del pitched the idea of supplying Grease with drugs and setting up a third 'line' of income for the group beyond the local cannabis and cocaine sales – economic diversification that offered them greater resilience. Bob and Billy did not like it, not one bit, and although they could easily have used their voice and influence to shut it down, the group was a democracy and they voted with the majority. In the end, heart won out over head – Grease was a friend and friends deserve a second (or third, or forth …) chance. As Bob explained: "I had been unsure what to think. You know, Grease man, he is always going to be Grease. He can't help that, [but he] is still our boy. It is a hard one. Del wanted him in; they are best mates. I am best mates with Del. Grease as well. Fuck it. You know. What you [going to] do?"

Midnight run

Our second case study also deviates from the 'standard story' of county lines, though it is very much rooted in violence and vulnerability. It starts late one night at a newbuild three-bedroom family home in the suburbs of Glasgow.

"Come on, get up", Amy said, waking her youngest daughter Claire. "We need to go. Now."

Amy's ten-year-old son Mark, Claire's older sibling by two years, was already wide awake and standing by his mother's side in Claire's bedroom.

"Where are we going mummy?", Claire asked.

"We need to go to see your gran. She wants us to see her", muttered Amy, not paying attention because she was rifling through Claire's drawers and dumping her clothing into bags.

"Do as mum says Claire, get ready", Mark said. The tone of Mark's voice told Claire he was not joking.

"Where are we going again?", asked Claire, peering out the window from behind the roller blind. It was still dark outside. Claire could see street lights in the distance.

"Gran's, Claire", said Amy.

"But why? It's still night-time. Where's dad?", asked Claire.

"Out. He will meet us there later. Hurry now."

Claire sat down on a little chair in her room, which was part of a set, including a table and another chair, though that one was missing a leg. Her dad had smashed it a few weeks ago during an argument with Amy over money.

Arguments were usually about money in this house, or so Claire thought. In reality, the family had plenty of money. The arguments were really about what the money was spent on. Claire's dad John never really liked Amy going out much, and Amy never really liked to be kept in much. Whenever Amy left to visit friends or went out for a night on the town, John got jealous – and angry.

However, the root of John's anger and trust issues was much deeper. John was raised by heroin addicts and his dad ruled with a rod of iron. He was violent with John growing up and would barter John's childhood possessions for drugs. Christmas presents would disappear within hours of unwrapping, exchanged for the next high. The irony was that heroin had robbed John of his childhood but was now how he made a living – a good one too. He was the master of heroin by selling it. Yet, the stresses of the illegal drug trade were also why John routinely smashed up his own house in fits of rage or held a knife to Amy's neck and interrogated her every move whenever she came home late.

Amy never cheated on John and never did anything to put him at risk. She loved him. However, his actions that night were the final straw. She had gone to visit her brother Echo, the one John did not like because he would stand up to him, and John was livid.

"You are fucking leaving me, eh?", he asked her.

"What? No, course not", Amy replied.

"Why you seeing Echo then? He hates me. What did you talk about?"

"He doesn't hate you, John. Just doesn't always like how you treat me."

"Treat you? How's that? Eh? How do I treat you?"

"Fuck off John. Don't start."

"Start what?"

"You know. Start."

"WHO YOU FUCKING TALKING TO YA DAFT BITCH!"

Domestic violence can be a slow, intensifying process – a murder in slow motion that takes the soul long before it leaves the body. The previous exchange was often how the dialogue between John and Amy escalated. Amy's friends in similar situations of domestic abuse would stop there. They would apologize or just sit quietly and hope their abuser would simmer down, though he rarely did. However, Amy was different: she never backed down from a fight, even a fight with a man. She had been like that since she was a teenager, after her mum began to deteriorate through illness and Amy was forced to take care of her younger siblings. Amy was tough, resilient and so accustomed to the coercive control of men that she felt almost numb to it. Amy's coping strategy was to fight back, even goad her abuser, to prove she was not afraid.

John jumped off the sofa and slapped Amy, knocking her to the floor. Amy then picked herself up and grabbed a mug half-full of coffee from the table. She launched it at John and it exploded off the side of his head, knocking him to the ground and turning the carpet around him a darker shade of beige.

"Ya fucking cow", John barked.

Although in shock, and slightly scared, Amy mocked him.

"Ya fucking wimp. Barely touched you. Next time it will be right in the face, you touch me again."

John exploded. He unleashed a frenzied attack on Amy, punching her repeatedly. She dropped to the floor and John leaped on top of her. He clasped his hands around Amy's neck and began to squeeze.

"DAD! DAD! ENOUGH!"

It was Mark. John and Amy's 10-year-old son had been standing there the entire time. Not for the first time, he had watched his mother beaten to a pulp and nearly strangled to death.

John stopped. "You, back to your room."

Mark froze. He was afraid – and ashamed. He had been told in school many times by teachers and visiting police officers that domestic violence must be stopped, but here it was and he could do nothing about it.

"Now!", John shouted.

Mark still did not move. John interpreted this as rebellion, so he slapped his son hard across the face.

"Room."

Mark sobbed, clutching his cheek. His dad had never hit him like that before.

"Fuck you doing, John?", Amy said, rushing to her son's aid. "You fucking animal", she snarled. "Get out. Just get OOOUUTT!"

John grabbed his coat and did as he was told. Stepping out into the cold winter air, he realized he had become the one thing he swore he would never be: his father – someone who hit his children.

Likewise, Amy had sworn that if John ever hit the kids, she would leave. The time when John smashed Claire's chair off the ground and the leg broke off and accidentally struck Mark, cutting his head, was the closest she had come to date. However, this was different. John had hit Mark so hard that Amy feared it had broken his jaw. She had no patience to wait for John's inevitable, manipulative, pitiful apology; instead, she called her mum and told her she was finally coming home.

Amy had barely hung up when her phone rang again. It was her brother Echo.

"That fucking wanker hitting you again? I am coming over. He's getting stabbed."

Mum could never keep a secret. Echo and his best mate James, Amy's first boyfriend when they were teenagers, were already in the car en route. This accelerated Amy's packing, and by the time Echo and James arrived on the scene, Mark and Claire were already bundled up in the car and she was locking up the house to leave.

"That prick hit you? Hit Mark? He's a fucking dead man", Echo said.

"We are leaving. Just leave Echo. Just leave", Amy pleaded, though she knew it was pointless. Echo was stubborn and he hated John, always had. In fact, Amy first met John in a nightclub because he had punched Echo in the face with knuckledusters. She should have known better than to date a man who had knocked out her brother in a fight.

Amy got in the car and drove to her mum's. Echo and James stayed, and when John got home, they ambushed him.

For the sake of the children

'Tap, tap' on the window, then 'thud, thud, thud' on the door. "Fucking open up it's the police", shouts a voice through the letter box.

Jack was never one to shy away. Police or not, he did not like waking up to the sound of his door and windows getting put in. Admittedly, it was three in the afternoon, but still, Jack reserved Sundays for sleeping.

"Oi! Lay off, lay off on the door, eh", Jack yelled, flying down the stairs. Jack lived in the top flat of a four-in-a-block cottage-style home with a shared communal garden.

He opened the door dressed only in a pair of shorts. Standing there was Grease, someone Jack had not seen in over a year.

"All right mate, happening?", Grease said, walking in, suitcase in hand.

"Fuck all man. Good to see you, but would be better if you weren't smashing my windows to get in", Jack replied, tired and cranky.

"Fuck up, or next time it will be your jaw." Same old Grease. He lost way more fights than he won, but Grease always had a way of turning any conversation into a test of strength and manhood. He leaned over and playfully grabbed Jack. The two wrestled for a minute until Jack admitted defeat and asked to be let up. This was Grease's way of establishing dominance over anyone smaller or younger than him. He would call them a "gimp", "a wee lassie that couldn't fight" or "Grease's bitch" before releasing them.

"Fuck sake Grease, you been putting on the weight, eh? Almost broke my back sitting on me there", Jack joked, trying to save face. Glasgow lads love to make fun of one another. However, it was true, since Mary left, Grease had piled on the pounds drinking beer and eating fast food at unsociable hours.

This was the perfect segue to talk about Jack's sister Mary. Grease explained that he had moved to A-Town to reconcile with her, "for the sake of the children". This was mostly true, but Grease now admits that he was also running away from some drug debts and was highly motivated to set up his own drugs line. Mary was living with Jack now, which made Grease's showing up on their doorstep out of the blue rather awkward:

> 'Mary went back to [A-Town] and moved in with her wee brother Jack. 'Cause you need to be in the place, really, to get a house from the council, and living though in Glasgow, she had no chance of getting one. Not that many really come up. We had split aye, but no really. We are always on and off like that, get me. Just the way we run, but it works for us two. I knew she was going, [and we] had already spoke about it a few times, me going up there. Her cousin was going to set me up with a job in the local hotel that way. She said she was going. I said I wasn't but then I decided to go. Not really wanting to be without her, know? Don't matter where we lived. Aye, I got there [in A-Town] and spoke to Jack. She hadn't said I was going to be moving in with them, but he knew I was on my way up. Was awkward, aye [laughs]. I basically just said, "Look mate, I need to be here for them. They are my family and I'm no living in a different house from them." Jack is sound, but he

gets it. Saying that he never really had the option but [laughs].' (Grease)

The preceding statement provides insight into Grease's manipulative personality and parasitic relationship with Mary and Jack. Mary and Jack had always been close, and Jack was always willing to help his sister out, even if it meant inconveniencing himself. Grease knew this; thus, he followed Mary to A-Town. Grease states that his "on and off" relationship with Mary "worked for them", but the fact that Mary relocated to A-Town to raise her children suggests that she saw it differently. Still, Grease had no intention of "living in a different house", which put pressure on Jack to accommodate him. The play fight when he arrived was another way of Grease stamping his authority on the situation.

By effectively commandeering a home in which he was not particularly welcome, Grease had created a local base of operations. He failed to turn up for his job interview at the hotel, which Grease claimed was a "waste of time" because it was a zero-hours contract. He sponged off of Mary and Jack for a while, who themselves were living largely on benefits, until they were eventually desperate enough to listen to Grease's financial proposal to sell drugs in A-Town on behalf of the gang back in Glasgow. The plan was in motion.

Moving out and moving on

It had been nearly a month since she had packed her bags and left, and Amy had not seen John once – this despite John's many text messages apologizing and accepting that he fully deserved the beat down that Echo and James gave him the night she fled. Amy was moving on, so much so that she was starting to reconnect with a casual acquaintance, Charles, on Facebook, someone she had spent time with when she was younger. Amy wanted to find a person who would love her right, and Charles had shown interest. He asked if they could meet again in person.

Amy got her mum to watch the children, and one night when they were asleep, Amy left to take a late-night ride in Charles' black Audi TT. They drove to the local McDonalds, got some food at the drive-through, then parked in the carpark to eat it. Amy and Charles were talking when suddenly Charles noticed a car pull up behind them, flashing its lights.

"Who's that flashing?", Charles said, blinded by the light.

Amy recognized the car. Her heart sank. "Just drive. It's my ex. That's his mate's car."

Charles reached down to turn the key in the ignition when a man suddenly appeared at the window. It was John.

"That's my bird mate", he said.

"Sorry about this", Amy said affronted. "Please, just drive."

John threw open the driver's side door. It was unlocked.

"Get the fuck out now", John said, yanking on Charles' jumper. Charles froze.

"GET OUT!", shouted John, slapping Charles around the head several times. Charles scrambled out. "Fucking calm it mate", he pleaded.

"I ain't your mate", John replied. "You fucking doing with my bird, eh?"

"I didn't know. She said she was single."

"Well, she's not. So, fuck off", John said.

John's not an imposing man, but he is intimidating. Rumour has it he was involved in the murder of a young lad as a youth, and as an adult, he was linked to the disappearance of another male who later turned up dead. 'For protection' as a drug dealer, because drug dealers must be 'self-enforcing' (Densley, 2013: 64), John occasionally carried a firearm. Charles was out of his depth.

"You need to get out", said Charles, turning to Amy.

This was a serious turn-off for Amy. She had always been attracted to "dangerous" men who would stand their ground. That was not Charles.

"Fuck off then", she said, leaping out of the car and storming off. John gave chase as Charles dove back inside his Audi and sped away.

"Where you going? Who the fuck that guy, eh?", John inquired.

"Fuck off John. We aren't together. I will see who I like. As long as it's not you."

"Wait, listen", John pleaded. Then something clicked for Amy.

"Wait a minute, why you here? You don't even come here. How'd you know I was here? Are you hacking my Facebook?"

"No", John said.

He was lying. For weeks, John had been monitoring Amy's social media accounts and her correspondence with Charles, and that night, he had used the Find My iPhone app synced to their kids' iPad to track her down. It was then that Amy realized that she was not safe even at her mum's house. John was too close.

Amy called a female friend who lived close by to pick her up. On the drive home, this friend mentioned that a distant relative was renting a house out in B-Town, miles away from the city and all its problems. It solidified in Amy's mind the need to flee Glasgow and move as far away from John as possible.

The only problem was that Amy needed money to make a fresh start. Amy had played the dutiful housewife for years while John was the breadwinner of the family, but money was also one of the many ways by which John had controlled Amy. It was not always that way. Earlier in her life, Amy had stored and sold drugs, and run errands for her uncle, a wholesale drug dealer. Her dad was not around and her mother was disabled, so this was her (and her uncle's) way of helping out the family, especially after one of Amy's brothers went to prison. Amy was always the brains of the family and her brothers were the brawn. Eventually, Amy got so good at the drugs game that she started her own business independent of her uncle, though he remained her main supplier. Amy graduated to wholesale supply of Class A drugs like cocaine and heroin,[1] as well as large quantities of cannabis. Her two youngest brothers set up cannabis grows and factories in rented homes and industrial units, and with such a large family, they had a lot of friends to sell to, who, in turn, became the retail arm of the operation.

After Amy met John and became a mum, however, she turned the business over to her brother Echo. Echo was a natural "fuck-up" she told us, who got unnecessarily involved in direct retail sales and started fights with customers and rival dealers. This affected the business in many ways, and while money remained good, it was an ideal time for Amy to take back control of the reins and start making her own money again. She talked to Echo and slowly began to assume control of the family business, mending fences, which was fine for Echo because he hated the politics of the underworld and just liked "playing gangster".

Amy eventually rented the house out in B-Town, paying cash directly to the owner so none of it went through the books. Amy enjoyed getting away from the hustle and bustle of the city. Country life was different, and quiet, and she finally felt a safe distance away from John and from all the enemies her brothers had made over the years. Still, working remotely, she noticed something. First, she was not alone. Other known offenders in the area had migrated from Glasgow, the Central Belt, even Edinburgh, to avoid drama in the big city. They were now living relatively peaceful lives despite existing ties to big-city organized crime. Second, demand for illegal drugs was high in the area, but supply was maintained by just two families, small timers who dealt directly with customers. This gave Amy the idea of taking over the drugs trade in the town and using it as a base to begin to supply the local villages too. She could not do this alone, in part, because she wanted to remain discreet, so she invited Echo to stay with her, which he regularly did anyway, scope the place out and get to work in the new village doing what she had always done best – making contacts and making money.

Concluding remarks

The findings from this chapter contest the 'standard story' that all county lines start with gangs shipping young recruits off to places where they have no prior knowledge to sell drugs on behalf of their puppet masters stationed hundreds of miles away. Amy and Grease migrated from their 'hub' city of Glasgow to their 'county' sites in A-Town and B-Town, respectively, not at the direction of gang leaders, but for social or family reasons. Much like Maxson (1998) found 25 years ago in the US, crime opportunities and drug market expansion were secondary motivations for gang proliferation and gang member migration. Further, these were permanent residential moves for Grease and Amy, not short trips or temporary relocations to sell drugs. B-Town, in particular, became a drug destination spot almost by happenstance.

Our two county lines case studies are anchored in domestic strife. Grease moved to A-Town principally to reconcile with his estranged partner. Amy moved to B-Town mostly to escape her abusive one. Both cases speak to the vulnerability and violence that are central to the standard story of county lines, but because the lives of adults are complicated, the constrained, complex and contextual nature of criminal decision making is emphasized. Both cases highlight that strict rational-actor frameworks only get us so far in understanding the aetiology of county lines (Cornish and Clarke, 1986), even if 'opportunity' is something that our interviewees do eventually seize upon (Clarke, 2012).

THREE

Joining the Line

Introduction

The standard story on county lines emphasizes the exploitation of children by adults and the role of women as victims and passive participants within criminal economies. Our case studies offer new insights into the participation of adults in county lines, including women who fully embrace the life of deviant entrepreneurship. The absence of legitimate opportunity in communities already punctuated with drug crime and addiction pushes people to start or join a county line, while at the same time the prospect of fast and easy money and an escape from the doldrums and dangers of city life pulls them in.

£500 a week

With Grease now settled in A-Town, it was time to build his drugs line. He started by calling his mother's landline phone and asking to speak to his aunt. He did not really need to speak to her, but that was his cover to get to her grandson, Robert. Direct contact with Robert would have seemed 'sus' that Grease was up to something – his aunt was well aware of Grease's wheeling and dealing. She had always liked Grease, but she did not want her 16-year-old grandson following in his footsteps.

"All right wee man, happening?", said Grease into the phone.

"All right Grease", replied the young voice of Robert.

"You been doing good, aye? Your gran was saying you've been getting into a wee bit of bother round the scheme, aye?", inquired Grease. Rumour was that Robert had been running with the wrong crowd in the public housing complex lately.

"No really, mate. She's freaking out. You know the way it is."

"Sound. You need any cunt sorted out, though, just give your big cuz a call, aye?"

"Aye Grease, no problem."

Enough small talk, Grease got to the point. "What you been doing anyways for money? You want to come out and see me out here for a bit, eh?"

"I don't know man. I have school coming up after the break—"

Grease quickly cut Robert off. "Fuck that. Pft, school. What you want to go back to fifth year for? You won't get nothing from it. Boy your age should be working. Grafting. Earning some money, fuck sake." Grease appealed to Robert's fragile masculinity. He told him school was for "poofs" and unemployment was for "losers". Then he went in for the kill. "You know I would have you out here, bring in £500 a week, easy. Who else your age is doing that? No one. Come out and see me. Even for a bit, aye."

"Let me think about it, eh", Robert demurred.

"You not needing the money, no? Here, take my number", said Grease.

Robert jotted down Grease's mobile number.

"Mind letting me know by the end of the week? Opportunities like this don't hang around." This was Grease's way of pressuring Robert, making him believe that other prospects were waiting in the wings. "By the way, mind, call me over WhatsApp. Do not be texting me either. Phone me", Grease added. This was to evade law enforcement agencies. WhatsApp's end-to-end encryption ensures only you and the person you are communicating with can listen to what is sent, and nobody in between, not even WhatsApp.

Robert was left to ponder Grease's offer. £500 for a week's work was certainly tempting. However, Robert had prior experience working with what his gran called "wrong ones" like Grease. He bought cannabis from him a year earlier on 'tick' or credit, but when it came time to pay, Grease added £20 to the price for 'late fees'. On another occasion, Grease sold him cannabis that was slightly under advertised weight, which got Robert's back up and made him feel Grease was a bit of a charlatan.

Robert visited his best friend Graham for advice. Graham lived a stone's throw from Robert, who entered the house through the backdoor to avoid waking Graham's dad, a labourer who worked shifts and could be a bit of a tyrant when he was tired.

"What's happening mate?", asked Graham, who was lying shirtless in bed playing video games.

"Nothing man. Just thought I would come round for a wee game of FIFA. Had to get out the house. My gran was busting my balls 'cause my cuz Grease phoned me."

"Aye, what that dick want?", said Graham. Graham had never liked Grease; he thought he was a bully who was always trying to show off what little he had.

"Asked me to go see him in A-Town. He is there now. Moved back there with the missus."

"You going to go? Fuck he want you there for. Place is a desert", quizzed Graham.

"See him. Do a few errands. Get some money in. He hasn't really said but asked me to call him later", Robert replied. "Would only be for like a week or two. He is offering me £500 a week. I need the money mate. I can get a new set of trainers. Them ones are talking to me now", Robert joked, looking over at his well-worn shoes parked at the backdoor. "And it would get me a wee run-around." Like most 16-year-olds, Robert wanted a car.

"Long as he is going to pay you, go. Fuck it. Why not. Two weeks' work for a grand is good", Graham came back.

That was it. Robert's mind was made up. As he explained to us:

> 'Suppose I was thinking about the money. I did think, "This is bad news." But I grew up in a house with my gran. She wasn't working really. She only did a part-time job cleaning and helping out in a school in town. I think, in the end, it comes down to: do I need the money or what? I did. ... I remember seeing [Graham's dad]. It was winter and we were just playing the computer in Graham's. He was up late at night, came into the room eating a cold dinner that had been sitting on top of the microwave for hours, pure-stating chicken. It looked shit but was good because we had been eating it earlier. I was always at Graham's for dinner. His mum would say if I wanted to come and eat. But [Graham's dad] was up pure late, eating shit food, and came in and seen Graham for five minutes before having to go to work. Remember looking outside and thinking "pure freezing out there", and he was going out in it. His car was broke as well, and he didn't have money to get it fixed that week and was going for the bus. I remember thinking, "I never want to do that. I never want to be that. Working all the time, missing life." He is a good guy. Pure grafter as well. It's a shame. No[t] like he doesn't get good money. He does. But it's not enough, you know.'

Robert wanted the one thing every boy wants but so few men ever achieve in these parts: disposable income – '"Fuck you money'. You know, enough money that you can pretty much do whatever the fuck you want." Watching Graham's dad work hard "all the time" and "missing life" for little financial reward solidified in Robert's mind that Grease had made him an offer he could not refuse. Grease drove down to Glasgow the next week to pick up some clothes and other belongings from his mother's house – and to pick up Robert.

Echo's chamber

At first, Echo had little interest in joining Amy in B-Town. He visited from time to time, bringing gifts for the kids and playing 'cool uncle' when he did, but he was sceptical that this small town of 2,000 people was the hidden, lucrative marketplace Amy made it out to be. B-Town also lacked the nightlife and entertainment that a young man like Echo was accustomed to.

However, things changed one evening when Echo was out on the town in Glasgow with his friend James and younger brother Paul. The three of them bumped into members of a rival outfit, and after a brief altercation, Echo, James and Paul were thrown out of the nightclub by the bouncers. They moved on to another venue only to get into another punch-up, which put Echo in the hospital. Later that night, Paul was attacked outside his home by the same group of lads. He was slashed across the side of his head with a knife and permanently scarred. Echo and Paul's younger brothers retaliated, beating the knifeman and dropping a slab of concrete on him. However, this only escalated things further, earning one of the brothers a fractured cheekbone.

Amy visited her battered and bruised brothers in the hospital the next day. There is a gang intervention charity in London called Redthread that does what Amy did next, using the daunting environment of a busy hospital as a 'teachable moment' or catalyst for positive change (see Redthread, no date). She leveraged the 'pull factors' of life in B-Town, namely, the opportunity to make money selling drugs without all the usual drama, precisely when the 'push factors' of intense crisis and serious injury were heightened (Roman et al, 2017). It worked. Echo agreed to move in with Amy, and Paul agreed to move out to the Glasgow suburbs and stay away from the city long enough for tensions, which had reached boiling point, to simmer down.

Once he arrived in B-Town, Echo began frequenting the two local pubs in the area. He sold drugs there, mostly cocaine, to younger, recreational users who were regular pubgoers. Echo is charismatic, a storyteller, and he soon became popular with the locals. However, what he needed was an outlet for heroin sales because the nature of opioid addiction created a steady income stream. His big break came when he met Peter, a local man with a substance use disorder. Echo met him on the street. "You looking for a bit of white, eh? Or brown, you know?", he said. Peter initially declined, as he was trying to stay clean, but Echo gave him his phone number and told him to call if he changed his mind, and sure enough, Peter did.

"Who is this?", said Echo.

"It's Peter. You said I should–"

"Peter my man. How are you? You looking to score, aye?"

"Aye mate, well not for me, for my pal." Echo had heard this lie a thousand times before. The drugs obviously were for Peter.

"Sound mate. Where you want to catch up? Text me your address."

"No, it's fine, I can meet you–"

"Don't be daft mate. I am out anyway. Tell me your address and I will drop off."

Peter was reluctant to let Echo know his address, but he lived alone in a one-bedroom flat, and in a small town like this, he knew Echo could easily find him anyway; all he had to do was ask around.

Echo arrived on the scene and immediately smelled an opportunity.

"Nice mate. Got a wee pad", said Echo. "Who's here? You got a missus?", he probed.

"Nah mate, just me. My daughter use to come see me. Well, her mum dropped her off, but they don't live here now so."

"Aye. I hear you. See the reason I wanted to come and see you mate was to put on a wee proposal. See, I was thinking that a man like yourself is a good person to know. Rather than me selling you this bag for your mate, how about I just give you it, you give him it for cash, and you keep the cash for yourself."

"Aye that sounds good, but what about paying for it?" Peter was confused.

"Aye rather than you paying me money, do me a favour. Hold on to some gear for me and I will get it at a later date. It would only be for a week, two tops."

Peter pondered the offer and reluctantly agreed. He had held onto illegal goods before, even sold drugs once or twice to pay for his own habit, so he was not too far out of his comfort zone — yet.

The next day, someone showed up at Peter's flat with a package. It was heavy, several kilos at least. Peter was told it was for Echo.

Two days later, some more people showed up at his flat "looking for two bags" to "score".

"What?", replied Peter angrily. "Fuck off? You have the wrong door."

"But we were given this address", one of the lads replied.

"What? By who?"

"Paul."

Paul was, of course, Echo's younger brother. He was now also in B-Town, casually making friends with local heroin addicts.

Peter called Echo for an explanation. "Echo mate, what's going on here? I've just had two guys at my door looking to score."

"Mate, you serve them?", asked Echo.

"What?! No", Peter replied, confused.

"Fucking why not, eh?", Echo answered, aggressively.

Peter was taken aback. Unsure how best to respond, he pled his case with Echo that he was no drug dealer and he wanted the packages removed from his house immediately.

Echo showed up at Peter's flat the next morning with his brother Paul and best mate James. After some discussion and some not-so-subtle persuasion, it was agreed that Peter would keep the package and sell what was in there in exchange for enough money to pay his rent and a daily hit of heroin for him and his friends. They unwrapped the package together to reveal one large bag of heroin, some equipment for weighing and bagging product, several prepacked bags, which varied in weight, and some other bags filled with prescription opiates and ecstasy tablets.

Over the coming days and weeks, Peter's flat became a destination for drug sales facilitated by Paul, who took orders via his 'burner phone', a cheap, prepaid mobile phone that was easily destroyed or discarded when no longer needed. Paul spent most of his time socializing with drug users, and cultivating contacts in the town, which resulted in him forming a relationship with a young woman, a recreational drug user. Like Paul, she used drugs periodically rather than problematically. Paul moved in with her but maintained his own home in Glasgow, which was occasionally used as a 'crash house' for his friends and brothers, a 'stash house' for drugs and a 'safe house' for criminals on the run from the police. Paul became the de facto courier for the county line.

Greasing the wheels

It had been a few tense nights. Jack was feeling the pressure of Grease living in his house, eating his food, and sleeping in his bed. He had to constantly remind himself that he was doing this for his sister and her kids. It helped to look at her sitting across from him on the three-seater sofa with the children on her lap. Still, the house felt crowded, and Grease's brash nature and failure to clean up after himself, even take out the rubbish, was wearing on Jack. Not to mention that there was now another mouth to feed — a teenager, Robert. Jack didn't know Robert, and when he asked Grease why the young boy was there, Grease said simply, "Come on mate, it's my cousin. He's only here for a week or so."

Jack had little privacy left, to the extent that when he visited his best friend Allan the next morning, Grease and Robert tagged along. However, this was about more than simply passing the time together — Grease knew Allan was key to winning over

Jack and getting his county line started. Jack was a few years older than Allan, but Allan was much more of a risk taker. The two of them grew up together in the same neighbourhood. Allan still lived with his mother, who, at this time, was grieving the recent death of his father. Allan's daily mood – and drug consumption – was often contingent on how his mother was coping, but today he was sober and in good spirits.

"How's it going Grease? Long-time no see, ma man. Jack said you were coming up to stay here", was Allan's opening gambit.

"Good mate, happening, eh? Aye, I am living here now. In with Jack me and Mary are, but looking to get our own place soon", Grease replied.

Not soon enough, Jack thought to himself.

That afternoon, Grease initiated a conversation with the group. He wanted to move illicit drugs from Glasgow to A-Town, and he wanted Jack, Robert and Allan in on it. As Grease explained:

> 'I thought it made good business sense. [We all] need the money. Billy and Bob were offering us the chance to make some. All we had to do was set up a shop and get grafting. Make them money, take a cut and that was all. Jack wasn't pure happy about it, but fuck him, what's he going to do? Not let me make money for my family. He would have got knocked the fuck out and told to sit back, the wee shit. He couldn't keep me, know. ... Yeah sound, I asked Allan if he wanted in. He was down for it. He had always been a mad one, loved his drugs and good times, so course he was. Free gear [drugs]. Wee Robert's up here wanted to get cash in his pocket, impress the wee birds. He was into it. I had been trying to speak with Jack but thought best if Allan was into it, then he would be. They are close.'

Grease told them all about the newly merged gang back in Glasgow, what they were up to, how they were making money, and, most importantly, according to Grease, how they wanted him to set up a satellite base for them in A-Town and "flood the place with drugs". Grease somewhat exaggerated the status of the Glasgow-based organized crime group and his role in it, like any "manager" would do to make "his boys" feel at ease, he said. He told Jack, Robert and Allan that they would be strongly supported by a group with ready access to money, product, people, even firearms, and the boys were clearly impressed. (It is worth noting here that gun laws in the UK are among the toughest in the world. Very few people, even police officers, carry firearms, thus there is a certain criminal cachet attached to them).

Interestingly, Bob and the gang back in Glasgow offered us a different interpretation of events:

> 'I know [that] Grease went up there [to A-Town] giving it the "Big I Am". "I am hard as fuck, look at me." Love him, [but I'm] not stupid; I know what he is like better than most people, probably even [his girlfriend]. This is why I didn't want him involved in nothing. ... [The gang in Glasgow] trying to get started out and make shit work for everyone. Try to keep it low-key. He is up there yapping his mouth off. He would have had us all as Al Capone and Chopper Reid, you get what am saying?' (Bob)

Grease was really just practicing what Felson (2006) calls, 'big gang theory', making his group sound bigger and scarier than it really was. As Bob notes, while it was true they had drugs to sell and guns to enhance reputations and enforce sanctions, the boys were still trying to gain a foothold in the market in Glasgow, maintain good relations with other organized criminals and generally keep a low profile. Research (and Hollywood) consistently show that overt displays of violence and intimidation attract police attention and rival predation (see Von Lampe, 2016). They are "not good for business",

Bob said, and Bob very much viewed his gang as a 'business' and his colleagues as 'businessmen'. The problem was, Grease preferred playing the part of "hardman" or "gangster" first and businessman second, Bob said. In this regard, he was a lot like Echo from our other case study.

After the conversation at Allan's mother's house, Grease called Bob and arranged for a shipment of drugs to be sent to A-Town. Once in A-Town, the product would be stored at Jack's, though only temporarily until it was moved to an undisclosed lock-up or storage unit that Allan had access to. The product would then be sold from another person's house, who was yet to be recruited. The group initially considered using 'Junkie Barry', a known drug addict, but Robert rejected the idea:

> 'We was [discussing whose home to use] to sell drugs from, Jack [was] like "Let's just use Junkie Barry." [I was] like, "Hold up, fuck sake, 'junkie' is actually in his name here." He sounded pure dodgy. He might not have been, but fuck that, sitting about all day with some big guy that's full of the junk. Grease is giving it, "You're backed up mate." So fuck, I would have been killed by them in a mad junkie rage. What good is back-up if you're dead [laughs]. ... Allan but, he is sound, he phoned his wee cousin Sarah and she said to use Stacy. Stacy's mum had moved out and she was staying by herself, so it was good.' (Robert)

Allan's younger cousin Sarah knew her friend Stacy's mother had recently left the family home to take up a relationship with a man she had met online. Stacy was home alone. After a brief phone call, and after being sent a photo of Robert to see "if he was good looking", Grease joked, the teenage Stacy agreed to let the group use her mum's property in exchange for a small cut of the profits. Robert would sell the product directly from the address, which exposed him to significant risk, but he was young and there to make money, so he did not complain.

Allan took charge of cutting and bagging the product, and making sure people in the community knew it was available. Grease initially insisted on word-of-mouth advertising only – nothing in writing or on the Internet yet. Allan came up with the idea of using a burner phone for orders. He would give his number out for people to place orders, then contact Robert, and Robert would gather the product and meet clients at a prearranged spot to complete the transaction. If they ever sold out, Robert would call Allan for resupply. All Jack had to do was house the initial shipment of drugs, house the money and, of course, house Grease. Under the codename 'Jamie from the East Coast', Grease oversaw the entire operation, much like a pimp watches over his prostitutes. If anyone ever asked Allan or Robert whom they were working for, "Jamie" was the answer. Grease would collect money daily from Robert, pay the boys in A-Town weekly, then pay his Glasgow suppliers monthly in arrears, known colloquially as 'on tick', with interest, whenever they arrived in A-Town with the next package.

Peter pays the piper

Selling drugs from home put Peter in contact with a whole lot of people. Customers initially came to him via a burner phone, but as the clientele became known, "regulars" just approached the door directly. One such person was Susanna, a minor addict who frequented Peter's home looking to score but eventually got something more when the two of them formed a romantic relationship. For Peter, this was one upside of living in a stash house; another was access to drugs.

Echo was Peter's main point of contact in the drugs business, but their 'friendship' was very transactional. Paul was present when new packages arrived, but owing to his recreational polydrug use, he was less involved in the day-to-day sales and only got involved if Echo needed some 'muscle'. Coinciding with his own increased drug consumption, Paul was becoming more violent. He stabbed a young boy several times in the back over a passing comment in the street. He also battered one of Peter's closest childhood friends, again for little more than perceived disrespect. His reputation now proceeded him locally.

Echo was living full-time in the area, and through the drugs trade, he befriended a young male, Gordon, from a nearby village. Eventually, Gordon assumed the role of driver, making regular collections for Echo from Glasgow and couriering them back to Peter's home. Peter stored the drugs and Paul would visit to ensure that they were bagged properly and at the accurate weight. He would then collect the money, give it to Echo and Echo would give it to Amy. The drugs business was providing a stable, steady income for Amy, but Peter had no idea that she was the one pulling the strings, facilitating the exchange of drugs and money between Glasgow and B-Town and keeping Echo suitably supplied, but on a tight leash.

Peter and Susanna eventually started using more than their agreed allowance of drugs. Echo came to collect his money one week and found it short by several hundred pounds. He came back to the flat and pounded on the reinforced steel door – a recent security upgrade that he had installed, alongside a CCTV security camera.

Susanna opened the letter box. "Who is it?", she asked. "Collection or other?" This was her code for whether someone was a regular known customer or someone who had arranged by phone to collect drugs.

"It's Echo, open up."

Susanna paused. "Don't let him in", Peter whispered, hurrying down the stairs and pulling on some clothes.

"Open up Susanna, hurry up. I ain't going anywhere."

Susanna unlocked the door and Echo barged in, making a beeline for Peter.

"All right mate. You know why I am here eh?", he said.

"If it's about the money mate –", said Peter.

"Shut up, fuck-up. Have I not been good to you? Pay your rent, got your door done, got your furniture. Let you take your own gear from mine without paying. Even let you sell it to your mates to get you something extra. You fucked up", Echo said.

"Mate —"

"You're my boy, but you fuck me over, you get punished", Echo explained. Suddenly, Paul and Gordon walked in.

"Paul, do it", Echo instructed.

Paul marched forward and grabbed Peter's face and hair. He stuck his fingers in his eyes, then pulled Peter into a nasty headbutt. Peter crumpled to the floor in agony and then curled into the foetal position while Paul and Gordon kicked him repeatedly. In the end, Peter lost two teeth and suffered a broken nose and a bruised rib. He spent the day at A&E.

On his way out, Echo pushed Susanna against the wall and made it as though he was going to assault her too. Instead, he took several hundred pounds out of his pocket and placed it in her hand. The message was clear: this was not about the money, but the principle. It was about trust.

"Get this fucking place fixed up. It's a tip", Echo said.

Concluding remarks

This chapter introduced some of the more exploitative aspects of county lines drug dealing. It is well documented that county lines use young, marginalized and vulnerable individuals to ship and sell drugs, and this is part of what makes county lines so lucrative for older, adult criminals at the top of the food chain (Harding, 2020). In prior years, drug-dealing gangs or partnerships would purchase drugs at a certain level of the illicit drugs market and then move the product on to others at another level of the market, which essentially worked independently of one another. When gangs sell direct to customers, they typically use bona fide gang members or associates to do so (McLean et al, 2018; McLean, 2019), automatically tying them back to the group. County lines work slightly differently: here, the drugs gang extends their line of supply through a satellite – in this case, Grease or Amy. Having a true satellite in another location is something the existing literature on county lines often mispresents – the satellite is in the area long before product and people are ever sent back and forth. This is something our case studies highlight in unique ways. Both Grease and Amy serve as a buffer between the gang in Glasgow and the criminal enterprise in A-Town and B-Town, respectively, keeping local actors completely separate should arrests be made, while, at the same time, backing them behind the scenes.

Local actors are exploited in a variety of ways. For example, Grease gains entry to A-Town because his brother-in-law Jack feels compelled to help his sister and her children, as well as because he is intimidated by Grease. Grease claims he is just visiting, but his stay is starting to feel more permanent. Robert has more in common with the youngsters in our prior studies of county lines (for example, Robinson et al, 2019; McLean et al, 2020) who travel to other parts of the country to sell drugs for status gains, as well as to repay favours or drug debts. However, contrary to the 'standard story', Robert was never snatched from the streets or recruited out of the blue. Instead, he had existing family ties to Grease, who was mostly just exploiting Robert's financial and social standing as a teenager too old for school but too young (and too unqualified) for meaningful work. Robert had agency and was playing by the rules of the 'illegitimate opportunity structure' – classical criminology in action (Cloward and Ohlin, 1960). Likewise, young Stacy was an unemployed teenager attracted to Robert and living at home alone; thus, selling drugs at home with Robert felt like the right thing for her to do.

Allan's story of what Hesketh and Robinson (2019) call 'deviant entrepreneurship' is slightly different. Allan is dealing with the recent loss of his father, and as Deuchar (2009) found in his study of marginalized youth in Glasgow, at times of grief or personal loss (especially parental loss), young men are more suspectable to risky behaviours. Allan also has a history of drug use, and his inclusion in the scheme is key to Grease winning over a sceptical Jack. This is closer to the standard story of exploitation in county lines, but as an adult, Allan's situation does not qualify as *child* criminal exploitation, and that means it falls outside of the jurisdiction of many interventions shaped by that standard story.

Likewise, in B-Town, Peter's vulnerability is on full display. He is exploited by Echo, and his home is essentially being 'cuckooed' by Paul (Spicer et al, 2020). Peter was manipulated into joining the operation from the get-go and becomes more and more dependent on drugs and drug money the more and more exposed he becomes to violence and intimidation.

Finally, there is an important yet subtle gender dimension to this chapter. Both case studies show that the participation of women in organized crime is neither exceptional nor does it occur only in minor labour or subordinate positions. Amy in particular serves as an example of female leadership in county lines. She is neither a peripheral romantic partner and sex object exploited by a patriarchal male crime boss, nor is she an 'ideal victim' (Christie, 1986) of drug addiction and debt bondage. Amy is financially independent and very much in control of her body and mind. When Echo was being pushed out of Glasgow, Amy was the one pulling him over to B-Town with the promise of mythologized riches. And although she is now outnumbered by males, Amy still sits at the head of the table.

FOUR

Life on the Line

Introduction

This chapter walks readers through the first few days of drug sales in A-Town, emphasizing the tools, techniques and tactics our interviewees used to ship, store and sell drugs in the area. We discover that some drug dealers enthusiastically embrace the always-on culture of modern drug dealing and the use of smartphones and social media to reach customers, while others find delivery dealing a chore, and they only do it to keep up with consumer demands and customer preferences. The chapter also explores the dynamics of debt collection and conflict management in B-Town, and precisely why violence can be bad for business. These findings help flesh out the standard story of county lines by illuminating some of the dark corners of the practice and the strategic decision making that is usually shrouded in secrecy.

Opening day

Grease was nervous. He had not sold drugs before, at least not like this. He was now calling the shots and responsible for the wellbeing of others. The contract was two ounces of white, which would be sold 'pure', or uncut, at £100 a gram to help boost the group's reputation for quality, and as much cannabis as Grease felt he could shift. The reason for the limit on cocaine was that back in Glasgow, the gang were buying it at wholesale 'on tick' from several different suppliers, and they had to repay on time or face reputational risks – or, worse, violent repercussions. Cannabis was different because the gang were growing it themselves – they controlled the entire supply chain. Shipments would arrive in A-Town monthly. After two months, assuming everything was going well, the weight of cocaine would increase to half a kilo.

Bob was worried about leaving Grease in charge of so much cocaine given Grease's history of overindulging on the stuff whenever he was unsupervised. At the same time, Grease was worried about adhering to his "contract" with Bob. He did not like contracts because contracts meant "no fuck-ups" and eventually money would need to flow down the line back to where the drugs came from. While the people on other end of the line were his brothers and childhood friends, Grease knew they would hold him accountable, especially Billy. Billy was already sending him "friendly warning text messages", reminding Grease that there should be "no issues".

It was the day of the first shipment. Grease was waiting at the meeting point he had agreed with Bob the night before. Suddenly, he got a call on his burner phone. It was Bob again.

"Grease mate, change of plans. The new place that you are to meet the boys is [NAME]. You will see on Google Maps that across from the old industrial building there is an open car park. A country lane runs just off it. It is one-way. Go there now. Boys are waiting. Got ten minutes. Don't be late."

Grease got back into Allan's car (technically, Allan's mother's car), and they zipped over to the new rendezvous point, past fields and amateur football pitches, down overgrown country lanes. The ground underneath the track was full of potholes and the car ditched from side to side as they proceeded along. When they finally reached their destination and parked up, no one was there. Grease snapped at Allan for taking a wrong turn and getting them lost. A few moments later, he heard knocking on the boot of the car. It was Billy. Grease manually wound down the window.

"Alright mate, fuck you doing here? I had been expecting Paddy to do the drop", said Grease, curious as to why Billy was there. This was a risk for Billy, travelling with product, and usually something he would not do.

"Just thought I would come out. See what you have up here, that is all", replied Billy. "Open up."

Allan unlocked the door and Billy jumped in the back seat. He introduced himself using an alias, not his real name, then added, "Take me to the pad and let us see what you have."

"Head to Jack's mate", Grease clarified.

At Jack's house, Billy sat down with Grease, Jack, Robert and Allan, and gave them a little "pep talk". He explained that while Grease was their main point of contact, if there were any problems, Jack had permission to call back to Glasgow. As Billy recalls:

> '[I travelled to A-Town to] let the boys know we had their backs. [It is] good for morale. Wanted to see what Grease had going. You never know with that cunt. Seemed like he had them sorted. Got him to drive me round the place. Showed me the store house. Showed me where he would be getting wee Robert to sell from. Everything. I gave a bit of advice you know, tune it up that wee bit. The only thing that was wrong with it was who was running it [laughs]. Grease can always fuck shit right up.'

After a quick tour of A-Town and a few more words of wisdom, Billy got Grease to take him to the car he drove up in, which was parked not too far from the second rendezvous point. In the boot was Grease's package.

Billy handed Grease the duffle bag full of drugs and a new burner phone.

"This one is for you. It only has one contact in it. Another unused phone that only Bob will answer", said Billy.

"I already have a phone –", replied Grease.

"Fuck that. Bob said you use this one only. Delete his number from the other one and keep that one for your own boys up here. The only contact you have with us is Bob, and it's through this phone."

Billy then opened his wallet and gave Grease £100.

"Keep the other phone for just you and the lads. Get them all burner phones as well. No numbers Grease. I fucking mean it", said Billy.

He got in his car and just before he closed the door, he gave one last 'friendly warning'.

"Don't fuck this up mate. I'm not kidding. Any hassle you phone back and Big Del will be up."

Grease got back in his car and drove back to Allan's to drop off the product. The two of them then went to a local shop and purchased four new burner phones – one each for Jack, Robert and Allan, and another for Stacy so she could take incoming calls from clients. Next, they sorted the cannabis into large ounce bags, weighing approximately 28 grams each.

"Want to get high?", asked Grease.

Allan and Grease smoked some of the cannabis, taking pinches from each package to 'skim off the top' without making a noticeable difference to the weight. Then, they drove over to Stacy's house to drop everything off. It was around midnight by the time they arrived, banging on the door, high.

"Shut the fuck up. It is almost midnight. People are sleeping", Stacy said playfully as the duo walked in. While young, Stacy was not afraid to speak her mind. This was her first time meeting Grease.

"How's it going hen? Good to finally meet. Don't ever tell me to shut the fuck up again, but don't worry we are sound."

Stacy was unsure how to take this comment. Grease sat down on the sofa.

"Here hen. Here is the stuff." He placed the bag he had with him at the side of the couch. "It is all accounted for. The bags just need to be bagged properly. The cocaine into grams. Likewise with the weed. Robert knows what to do. He sold weed before for me in Glasgow. Bagged coke for his auld man as well. So, he will sort it. Don't you worry about it. But mind it's accounted, so no dipping it, or I will have to take your fingers off you", Grease explained. He was joking – or was he?

"I'll just put it in the cupboard. Robert can deal with it. Nothing to do with me. I don't touch drugs anyway, so I won't take it. Wouldn't even know who to sell to if you're thinking that", Stacy said reassuringly. She had met Grease's type before. Her mother had been in a few relationships with similar men.

Grease then took £50 and placed it in Stacy's hand.

"Good. Speak soon hen. Robert will be round tomorrow early bells, so get some shut-eye." Grease and Allan departed. Stacy went back to bed.

The week before Billy delivered that first shipment, Allan had put out word that "proper gear" would be coming into town and that if anyone needed anything, they should get in touch with him. The problem was that Allan did this before he got his new burner phone and so he was now being inundated with text messages from his friends and peers asking if he had anything in yet. There was pent-up demand in the area because, coincidently, a few months before Grease arrived on the scene, the town's main drug dealer, who, like Grease, was supplied from Glasgow and the West Coast, had landed in prison. Since then, the town had been dry. This was a happy coincidence, and Grease and the boys hoped to fill this gap in the market. Allan sent his contacts the following text message:

'ANYONE NEEDING WHITE, GREEN OR VALS GET IN TOUCH ON THIS NUMBER [phone number] FOR PRICES. SAY ALLAN SENT YOU FOR DEALS. DROP OFFS ARRANGED 24/7. ASK FOR JAMIE. NOTHING TO DO WITH ME SO DON'T TEXT ME BACK DIRECTLY. PASS THE NUMBER.'

Robert was already at Stacy's house when Allan sent out the text. He had spent an hour or so bagging the cocaine and cannabis, and counting out the 500 diazepam (Valium) pills Grease had handed him that morning before he left. Valium usually came in strips, but this was simply one large bag, which gave Robert the sneaking suspicion that these were street, or "fake", Valium put through a pill press, not stolen prescription tablets made in a lab. Grease also gave Robert scales, bagging equipment and an A4 piece of paper. On one side of the paper was a full price list of the drugs by weight and quantity; the other side had a list of sale prices and deal prices. Both sides were labelled with that day's date. Robert was advised to simply mark off each sale so that Grease could take a stock count at the end of the day and calculate the profit. Grease told him to be wary of large transactions because they increased the risk of robbery – something we document at length in McLean and Densley (2022). He also told him never to answer a phone call, but only respond to text messages.

"Mind wee man, you will get the text on the phone. Don't answer calls. Get Allan to agree the price and the amount to be sold, and you get it correct. It is on you to double check. Allan will tell them to bring the right money, exact, 'cause you don't want to be taking money with you to give change. Mark it off on the sheet and then go meet the guy", Grease told him.

At Stacy's, Robert weighed the cocaine and wrapped it into gram bags. He then bagged the "grass" grown in makeshift factories back in Glasgow into various quantities – eighth of an ounce, quarter-ounce, half-ounce, one ounce, which sold for £30, £50, £110, £200, respectively, slightly under market price in order to compete in a reasonably saturated cannabis market. He also sorted a few edibles made by extracting the THC from the cannabis, infusing it with butter, then cooking it into remoulded sweets. Edibles have grown in popularity ever since cannabis has been legalized or decriminalized in some parts of the world and the marijuana industry has diversified its product line (Doran and Papadopoulos, 2019).

By around 11 am, Robert got his first text message from Allan. Allan's phone is henceforth called the "hotline". This is the phone customers texted asking to score. Allan then forwarded the messages to Robert's burner phone using an encrypted messaging app. While somewhat inefficient, they did this to create distance between sales and delivery. Robert would reply to Allan when he was ready to meet the customer and schedule the rendezvous a few streets over from Stacy's house or at a nearby park. Allan would then text back confirmation and a description of the buyer, what he or she was wearing or driving, and so on, or some other distinguishing feature:

> 'Aye, first time I did a drop. ... I would lie if I didn't say I was a bit anxious. I wasn't anxious like thinking, "Oh, this guy is going to rob me" and stuff. I was worried more that I was going to fuck up. Like lose money, drop the drugs or just miss texts while I was out. I was worried more what Grease would be saying and the other guys. I wanted to do a good job. I know that sounds not right, sounds daft. But it was like a job I had been given. I wanted to do good.' (Robert)

The first sale, a quarter of cannabis, went well. Robert recalls the customer saying something about how he thought Robert would be older than he was and he replied, "Course not, they would have to pay me a proper wage then", and it broke the ice. No sooner had he made his first sale, however, did texts come in for two more. The first was a score bag or "SB", which is £20 worth of cannabis. At first, Robert thought it was a no-show, until Allan texted him to wait a little longer:

> 'I was going to leave and this car comes speeding right up beside me asking, "You Jamie's boy?" Took me a few sec[ond]s to mind what the fuck he was talking about. Was wondering, "Who is Jamie?" Then I was like, "Oh, aye, Jamie, aye, that is me." He handed over the money. Just £20 if I remember right, aye, enough. I gave him the weed and he put the window up and fucked off. Tunes were blaring, pure out. Was a belter of a car as well. An

orange number to fuck; they would well get pulled by police.' (Robert)

As the orange car disappeared into the distance, 'Jamie from the East Coast' was definitely in business.

The next order, however, was a little disconcerting: 20 Valium pills to be dropped in a more remote location than before. Valium is an anxiolytic that is highly addictive for people with a history of a substance use disorder or substance dependence. On the streets, Valium and heroin go hand in hand, and heroin withdrawal can turn desperate people violent and unpredictable (McPhee et al, 2019; McLean and Densley, 2022). However, Robert's fears were unfounded. He sold the Valium to a group of teenagers at the park for recreational use. The only hassle he got was from Allan, who was being bombarded with text messages: 'GET A FUCKING MOVE ON. PEOPLE ARE BUSY.'

This is something the 'standard story' on county lines has failed to fully capture. The standard story implies that county lines drugs networks happily embrace mobile phone technology because it simplifies the drug-dealing process, eliminating the need to sell drugs on street corners out of telephone booths and in front businesses, or in communal social spaces like 'head pubs' and nightclubs (Doyle, 2018). At the same time, the phone eliminates some of the uncertainty in the sales process through knowing where to go to buy and what physical and verbal signals to send to figure out who is selling. Existing research also argues that gang leaders embrace mobile technology because it facilitates round-the-clock surveillance of their workforce, known as 'remote mothering' (Storrod and Densley, 2017).

However, what we see here are the ways in which mobile phones contribute to information overload and an 'always-on' work culture, meaning that employees are always accessible and on the clock, even in the drugs trade (Nixey, 2021). Furthermore, while those instant messages and extra hours may seem like a boon for productivity, they come at the expense of people's physical and mental health, meaning that, just like in the legitimate sector, they contribute to burnout. It is easy to simplify this by calling work on county lines inherently coercive and exploitative, but it is more complicated than that. For example, as Grease explained it to us, Robert had an easy job, and he was doing him a favour asking him to do it: "The job is a canter. Sit in a house all day wi' a wee tidy bird at your beck and call. Got a price list and stock checker all done. Get a text and you just go meet the dude, get paid and go home. Come on." Robert, however, saw things differently:

> 'Aye, it was a stressful time. I didn't like it. I am glad I met Stacy. At the time [I'm just] told, "Here, take this", a massive bag of pills. "Walk your way to this lassie's house and stay there until ten at night. You don't know this lassie but get her told that you're living there now." Heavy awkward. And, "Oh, aye, by the way, police might come burst through the door at any point of the day", and "Oh, aye, you might get set up and robbed or stabbed off any the guys you are going out to meet, but don't worry about it, it is sound." You get a bit of paper and keep stock and price lists on it. Phone doesn't stop buzzing. ... After all that shit I am putting up with, I get handed 300 at the end of the week. Seven days' work, 300 quid. I was promised 500, and I am thinking that is like nine to five or something. ... Yeah, [it did] raise to 500 after the coke started moving. First month we had fuck all but. ... I am indoors a full week, and I still had to buy my own food. Not like Grease was dropping me off dinners. Lucky Stacy was good and fed me.'

From Grease's vantage point at the top looking down, Robert's job seemed relaxed and well compensated, but from Robert's perspective at the bottom looking up, the job was anything but. This paradox, and the fact that Grease had ordered Robert to "take over the place" when he got to Stacy's but Stacy was nothing but nice to Robert, cooking him breakfast in the morning, for example, eventually drove a wedge between Grease and Robert as the county line developed.

Still, that first day, the group made several hundred pounds, mostly from cannabis sales but also one shipment of Valium and a gram of cocaine. Robert finally got back to Jack's around 11 pm.

"Fucking heavy graft that was today", Robert told Grease when he got in.

"Fuck off. Sitting on your arse. Drinking tea", Grease replied.

"It was. It is hard going. By the way, I am going to need a bike. Did Allan tell you?", said Robert.

"A bike. Why?"

"To get about. It is too much time to walk around the place", Robert explained, Allan's text message weighing heavily on his mind.

"Well, it can come out your money. But, aye, I will get you one", replied Grease.

Robert was angry about this. Billy had said that if any issues came up, Grease would take care of them. Robert did not think that a bike to help expedite sales and manage the stress of the endless barrage of text messages should come out of his cut. At the same time, he half expected Grease to buy him a £100 bike and then dock him £200 in wages so he could pocket the difference.

"Grease, it is okay. I will get my own bike. Do not worry about it", Robert said, before heading upstairs to bed. He was starting to realize that his stay in A-Town may be longer than the two weeks he had signed up for. Meanwhile, text messages that came through to the hotline during the night were, at first, met with a reply that shop was shut and would reopen again the next morning. However, as the texts continued to ping into the early hours, it was easier to just switch the phone off and leave them unanswered.

Dancing with danger in B-Town

Business was good in B-Town, and things were also going well for Amy personally. Her ex-partner John was serving a long stretch in prison for firearms offences, and that freed her to rekindle her childhood romance with James, Echo's friend, who came to visit from time to time. Amy's only real stress in life now was making sure people paid their debts on time, though that was really Echo's and Paul's domain, not hers.

One strategy the brothers employed was hanging around outside the local chemist, which was where heroin users would fill their medical prescriptions for methadone, a synthetic opioid used to treat drug addiction. That was where Echo found Rudy one afternoon:

"Rudy mate, you been avoiding us?", asked Echo.

"Nah, I just have not seen Paul around", Rudy lied. Paul was usually the one who collected the debts.

"You know where Peter stays though, eh?", Echo replied. Indeed, Rudy was one of Peter's regulars.

"I didn't think you wanted people there dropping by the house", said Rudy.

"Enough Rudy, enough. Your bill is doubled now. Pay it next week to Paul or Peter."

"Fuck sake Echo man. Where will I get that?"

"Either that or your house will be burned to the ground and your dad battered to death. Pay it. No joke."

Echo often added interest to unpaid debts, though he did so arbitrarily. There was no fixed percentage, just whatever figure he felt like adding at the time. Then, as Echo turned to leave, James leaped out from nowhere and punched Rudy in the face, knocking him to the ground. James kicked Rudy in the head several times for good measure, knocking him unconscious. Rudy paid his bill the next week after selling some of his dad's belongings and several other items he shoplifted at the local pubs in the village.

In another example, a female sex worker and drug user, Emilia, owed Echo several hundred pounds, which with 'tax' went up to £1,000. To pay her debt, she was "put to work" Echo said. One of his associates picked Emilia up and drove her to Glasgow for the weekend, where she worked the streets and had sex with men until she had paid her debt in full.

Such tactics as these ensured that most people paid in full and on time, and this meant the business only grew. Amy's group meets county lines criteria because it was a Glasgow-based outfit that, through the chance moving of one of its members, Amy, to B-Town, was able to move drugs from Glasgow to the region when her brothers went to see her. At first, her brothers sold drugs (primarily cocaine) recreationally to pubgoers and partygoers. Then, they started dealing heroin to addicts in the area, using locals, Peter at first, to store and sell the drugs. Packages were dropped and money collected. When Paul moved intermittently between Glasgow and the region, and Echo moved from Amy's house in B-Town to his own place in another large town in the region but still some distance from the town and villages in which they primarily operated, this expanded the line further.

The group still retained the services of Peter, but they opened up shop at two other locations in the region. They hired some of Gordon's teenage and young adult friends as drivers to do drop-offs to customers in the region who ordered cannabis and cocaine advertised over the Internet. A regional landlord then made three of his properties available to the group as stash houses in exchange for a cut of the profits. Eventually, the county lines were such that Echo and Paul spent most of their time driving across this vast, sparsely populated, rural area to move money, though they still had time for debt collection and handing out beatings for delinquent customers.

This rapid expansion of the gang's activities eventually brought them into conflict with another family-based drug-dealing group in the region. In truth, the feud had little to do with drugs and turf, but was rather about Echo's manners, or lack of them. One night, while out drinking at a local pub, Echo and James started selling drugs directly to other pub patrons. Amy had warned them about this, but as recreational drug users themselves, Echo and James dabbled in social and retail supply whenever the opportunity presented itself. Echo then got into a dispute over a game of pool and hit the youngest member of a rival drugs gang with a pool cue. The young lad called his dad, who showed up later with his three other sons to confront Echo. A fight broke out and James was punched out by the oldest sibling, while Echo was battered onto the floor. An eyewitness phoned Gordon to intervene, who arrived just as the family was leaving. Gordon waited in his car for them to cross the road then drove into them, tossing one of the brothers over the car bonnet.

The fight made local news, which "embarrassed" Echo. He took revenge by setting fire to a caravan parked outside the family's home. Three of the brothers retaliated by beating up Gordon and one of his friends. Echo, Paul and James responded by ambushing the second oldest brother and putting him in the hospital. The feud was reaching fever pitch and beginning to attract police attention, so Amy used a neutral third party, a well-known criminal associate of the most powerful organized crime group in the region – a group with national and international ties – to broker a peace deal between the two families. It cost her several thousand pounds to do this, but she knew it was the only way to stop Echo sabotaging the county lines she had worked so hard to build.

Dial-a-dealer delivery in A-Town

Much like mobile phones have rendered workers contactable at all times, permanently tethering people to their work, the 'always-on' culture has reached drug dealing. Waking up each morning to so many overnight 'hotline' text messages was a sign of unmet demand in A-Town, even an incentive to extend 'business hours', but it was also a source of anxiety for Grease. His first sales weekend was approaching and that meant even more texts were coming. Grease really did not want to be drug dealing 24/7, and Billy had warned him to be careful not to overextend himself and get caught up in direct sales himself. Thus far, Grease was abiding by those rules. He lived by the motto, "It is not what you know, but what you can prove" that counts. The fictitious 'Jamie from the East Coast' was a decent cover story, but more streetwise clients would not be fooled by Keyser Söze[1] forever, nor would the police if they ever started to dig into Grease's background.

Grease needed a way to satisfy the demands of ravenous consumers, but he could not use his own car or even Allan's mum's car for 'ring and bring drug services' (Søgaard et al, 2019) because it would clearly implicate them in the scheme. His solution was "hiring wheels", that is, paying someone for the use of their car and for the labour of driving Jack about town to drop off orders when and where they were needed. He called Allan: "Allan, it is me. Get a set of wheels mate. Any one you know that we can trust. Say you will give them money to taxi Jack about. Don't tell them it is Jack, so preferably someone that doesn't know him."

"Fuck sake mate. That is asking. Most people I know, know Jack, or at least of him", Allan said.

"I don't fucking care. Try it, eh. We need to keep what everyone knows about each other limited."

"Leave it with me", replied Allan.

"You have until the night mate, 'cause we are losing a lot of money not doing night deliveries, especially with the weekend coming up."

Grease felt bad about putting so much pressure on Allan and for snapping at him, so he visited him later that night. For all Grease's shortcomings, he usually apologized if he felt he went too far, and he knew it was the constant bombardment of text messages stressing him out, not Allan. Grease and Allan were hungry, so they ordered a takeaway from the local Indian restaurant. Some 40 minutes or so later, the food arrived. It was 11 pm. Upon answering the door, it dawned on Grease that although the restaurant itself was now closed, the drivers were still doing deliveries. In fact, some delivery drivers worked until two in the morning. That gave him an idea.

"Why not get a real delivery driver to do the drops? He will be working anyway and getting paid. We would just need to give extra money. And there are plenty around. It would give a cover story as well, least until about 1 or 2 am, why they would be out", Grease pitched Allan.

"That sounds good mate. I don't know any drivers, though; I don't get takeaways often."

"I do. I have been using this place across in [North Village]. I speak to the driver. He is cool. I will just ask him tomorrow", said Grease.

This was the plan. The following afternoon, Grease ordered a meal early and asked for the specific driver he had in mind. When the driver arrived with Grease's order, Grease put forward his proposal: an extra £50 a night to let Jack shadow the driver on his delivery route and make some drops on the way. The driver politely declined but offered up his friend who worked nights and weekends and might be interested. As Grease states:

> 'The boy was cool. He handed me the phone over to his mate. Somebody called Davey that worked a few shifts in the shop. I went on and was like "Alright mate, you fancy making some extra money for driving bout?" Said that he would need to pick up my guy about 8 pm at the weekend and just drive him about till he finished up at 1 am. Would give him £50. He wanted £60 plus the petrol money, so I was like fuck it then, here you go. Said that it would be a set £120 if he would take him out Monday until Friday but from 9 pm to about 1 am. The [takeaway] shop shut a bit earlier during the week, so wasn't sure if he would be up for it. Said he wanted

the Friday off [and the second] Monday. I said that was sound. ... We had ourselves a wee recruit to drive us about. ... Aye, I made sure he picked up Jack round the corner though, I didn't want him coming to the door. Got Jack told, "Fucking get him to drop you off where he got you. No[t] here [at the house]." Gave the driver a wee bung [tip] as well, £20 for his help, plus to keep his mouth shut and not tell the boy the address. Course, he would have, [but as long] as he isn't turning up at the house, I can deny it was me.'

Davey was 19 years old, had his own social house and worked cash-in-hand jobs doing deliveries in order to bring in some disposable income. This was undeclared, as he was a welfare claimant and his cheque paid the rent for the social house in full. He worked nights for the takeaways so he could still attend his job-centre appointments in the day, retain his claim and stay in compliance for his benefits.

Davey worked for two takeaway shops in the local area. One in North Village and one in A-Town. The shifts for the North Village takeaway were every Saturday, Sunday, Wednesday and second Monday. The shifts for the A-Town takeaway were every Tuesday, and he also covered the odd Thursday shift. In general, shifts were quiet between 9 pm and the last late orders just before closing time. This meant that Davey had plenty of time to collect Jack and work the shop's deliveries at the same time. This was around the time people were starting to order food online, curtailing cash transactions between the driver and the customer, and reducing Davey's cash tips. He was more than happy, therefore, to earn a little extra working for Grease.

To keep Davey at arm's length from the rest of the operation, Grease had Allan bag up some of the stock and drop it off at Jack's prior to Jack leaving to meet Davey. If Jack ever needed resupplying, he was meant to have Davey drop him off, but Jack admitted that they played fast and loose with some of Grease's clandestine rules: "Grease wanted us doing CIA tactics.

It wasn't the mafia. We would [often just] drive up, get out, blether away and have a laugh, and then we would go back to work. Allan would go his way."

The simple truth about most county lines is they are run by average young people, not James Bond super-villains. Average young people get antsy and bored and over time they get too comfortable, and that is when rules get broken. For example, despite Billy insisting the group keep mobile phone use to a minimum, as the business progressed, Allan, who was in charge of "logistics and advertising", wanted a better way to reach his customers where they were – on social media. Cheap burner phones were fine for text messages and phone calls, but he really wanted a phone that could edit video and photos and send messages via social media apps like Snapchat and WhatsApp. As such, Allan made the unilateral decision to purchase from his friend a second-hand iPhone, which, in turn, became the group's new hotline number.

It is worth noting that in B-Town, Amy also saw potential in smartphones and social media facilitating drug sales. She told Echo to have Gordon and Gordon's friends, who were local to the region and sold drugs in the surrounding small towns and villages as part of his 'downline' (Densley, 2012b), to use Snapchat from their mobile phones to entice customers with limited-time 'deals' and to post pictures of the goods on offer.

The two cases highlight that while some drug dealers, like Amy, enthusiastically embrace the always-on culture of modern drug dealing and the new digital means of reaching customers, others, like Grease, find delivery dealing a chore – and a risk – and they only board that train later, reluctantly. This shows that the 'standard story' of technology driving change in drugs markets is incomplete. The county line in A-Town started with cheap burner phones and regular business hours but was forced to adapt to keep up with consumer demands and customer preferences, not technology per se. You might say that what makes a county *line* a county *line* is not really the phone *line* at all, but the extended drug supply line with no credit limit to constrain the remote actors. The use of a single deal phone or elaborate social media messaging campaign was never an integral part of the plan for our interviewees, and the prospect of trading the portfolios of drug customers, held on phone SIM cards, never even crossed their minds. Even if they originally used a single deal line, our interviewees eventually used multiple phones for deals and changed the 'hotline' number on multiple occasions.

Concluding remarks

This chapter has focused largely on the A-Town group from the moment their first small shipment of drugs arrived to 'test the waters' through the first week of sales. The findings in this chapter highlight that there are several neglected aspects in the 'standard story' of county lines. The first is the logistics of drug distribution and the networks required to not only reach customers, but also deliver to them. The stereotypical county line involves young children sent on trains to traffic drugs up and down the country, but this only gets gangs so far because missing children traveling alone draw attention. Grease, of course, works with young people – Robert and Stacy are 16 and Davey is 19 – but it is Billy, an adult, who makes the first drugs drop, and he goes to great lengths to conceal his activities because he wants this to be an ongoing business venture, not a one-time deal. A child on a train is not a sustainable drug delivery mechanism, and putting a child on a train to transport thousands of pounds worth of cash and stash is not a savvy business decision. It is easy to say that gangs do not mind if shipments get lost because they simply charge this as debt, but our interviewees were adamant that supply chain issues can seriously undermine their credibility, especially in new and emerging markets. Drugs are time and money, and a criminal gang is not in the business of wasting time or losing money.

Another aspect of county lines that prior research has not yet captured to the same extent as we do here is the process of trial and error and learning from experience on the job (Robinson et al, 2019). It took Grease and his boys several attempts to set the line up properly, such as bringing in Stacy, additional recruitment for deliveries (Davey), the use of burner phones and even buying Robert a bike so he could get to his drops on time. The standard story of county lines is that big-city youth, by virtue of their big-city experience, are already all expert in this, but the current study suggests that this may be an exaggeration. Big-city youth, allegedly enamoured with routine knife carrying, will also lift a knife, and this has increased knife crime in remote, rural areas, some argue (HMG, 2018). As we see with Robert, however, he is aware that every call he attends is potentially fraught with danger, but he has not carried a knife – at least not yet. In the coming chapters, we see how this plays out for Robert and what factors influence his decision making.

The current chapter has further demonstrated that while child criminal exploitation is a legitimate major concern in county lines, Robert is not simply a passenger in the process, and he seems to know exactly what he is getting himself into. Likewise, Davey may be young, but he enters into the line of his own volition. In the end, the line also requires adult supervision *in the area*, not simply back in Glasgow. Grease is there to maintain order and oversee production. Stock checks are required, product needs moving and there is coordination involved. He also needs to keep his workforce happy in order to keep the line running daily – sometimes, something as simple as a takeaway meal is all it takes. This was something well noted by Billy, who showed up unannounced not only to make sure everything was on track, but also to boost morale and cement the idea among the younger individuals that they were part of something bigger than themselves. It is well recognized in military campaigns and operations away from home that the troops need motivating, which is why senior officers often visit (Britt and Dickinson, 2006). The same principles were applied here.

FIVE

Crossing the Line

Introduction

The prior chapters have looked at the initial planning involved in establishing county lines, the first steps of the operation, the challenges and opportunities, and some of the ways our interviewees managed personnel and product. This chapter picks up the story in A-Town several months later, when the county line is in full flow. This chapter is the point where pride and greed start to erode away trust within the group, and where conflict arises such that the gang back in Glasgow needs to intervene to prevent the group in A-Town from tearing itself apart.

What goes up ...

As the weeks progressed, the line was running about as well as could be expected. The gang in Glasgow had their man in place, Grease, who was their general in the field. Allan was working hard to ensure adverting and logistics were running smoothly, putting out deals on the hotline and over Snapchat, and likewise ensuring that drug shipments were stored and dropped off at Stacy's every other day for Robert to sell in daytime hours. Jack was handling the night shift, doing direct deliveries with Davey, and Robert now had a bike, a BMX he stole from someone's front garden and spray-painted in an effort to not get caught. He had studied the town map, learned the short cuts and was getting good at direct sales.

In fact, Robert had become quite friendly with some of the local youth in town, including the boys he sold Valium to on his first day. One of the boys, Adam, was Stacy's second cousin, and he recognized Robert when he stopped by Stacy's house one afternoon with his mother and eventually got Robert to bring him in on the line. Robert was now dating Stacy (which was no surprise given how much time they spent together) and basically living with her full-time. This helped assuage his gran's fears that Grease was the only reason Robert was still in A-Town. Still, Robert was young and insecure, and threatened by Adam's relationship with Stacy – second cousins could still date – which was another reason he doubled down on the drugs business:

> 'I didn't mind working. Long hours don't bother me. I missed my gran. I had [wanted to go] back to school, [but what job was] going to get half a grand in cash a week. I loved Stacy. I wanted to be with her. I didn't like being away from her. She will say it wasn't the case, but it was. Adam was sniffing about when I was away. Trying to batter in [to Stacy].' (Robert)

As Robert notes, the decision to work on a more permanent basis for Grease was not only about money, £500 a week, but also about his budding relationship with Stacy. While it was his decision to recruit Adam to the line to help with sales, Robert was wary of leaving Adam alone with Stacy.

Still, Robert did commute from time to time. The gang back in Glasgow delivered packages to A-Town once or twice a month, but with business booming, Robert was eventually permitted to transport small quantities of drugs from Glasgow to A-Town whenever he was down to visit his gran. As Robert told us:

> 'They had a boy for [doing drops in A-Town]. That was like every couple of weeks or something. I had nothing to

do with doing [runs from Glasgow to A-Town because] the guy always got money from Grease. I was never given money; only Grease. Would have like a few rolled balls of notes. ... There was £50s, £20s, tenners and fivers. Really what[ever currency was paid by the customer]. ... A few times, Grease would say I was to get a bag from whoever, once Big Del. Aye, Big Del said "not to look in" the bag. Course I was looking in [laughs]. Most I had to ever travel with was an ounce of [cocaine] and an ounce of grass. I took a knife that time, aye.'

Robert claimed an ounce of cocaine could last a fortnight, but Allan said that in an average month, "we moved just shy of a kilo of pure. We mixed the batch, so, yeah, did alright." Things were going well, but, unfortunately, in the drug trade, there's always a comedown from the high.

... Must come down

It was a weekend night and the hotline had been ringing off the hook. Cocaine was the best-seller, followed by cannabis. Jack and Davey would sell cocaine direct to partygoers and people looking to get high, then revisit the same addresses later to sell cannabis for the comedown. Grease's separate Valium operation was not particularly successful overall, but the young people and the heroin users on the estate where Stacy lived seemed to enjoy them. The young people would take them while consuming alcohol; the heroin users took them in-between 'hits'.

Jack and Davey had made a killing that night, so to celebrate, they went to visit Allan, who was having a little party at his house with his girlfriend and a few of her girl friends because his mum was away for the weekend. It was gone 2 am and the shop was shut for the night.

"Come on in boys, make yourself at home", Allan said when Jack and Davey arrived. The duo handed Allan the night's takings and Allan started to count it.

"Let's get some lines out, ah", said one of the girls, fully aware of Allan's business.

Jack hesitated. Grease had explicitly warned them about getting high on his supply and he was also worried about Allan, who had struggled with drug and drink problems in the past. Predictably, Allan was all-in, and egged on by the girls, Jack relaxed too, but he made them promise that they would pay in full for what they used that night.

Except they did not. Allan's party girls left without paying their tab. They claimed they would settle up with him next week, and in the meantime, Allan would cover it 'on tick'.

"Allan, I am not happy at those lassies. They were basically here for a free ride", Jack complained.

"What you mean? We invited them, didn't we?", replied Allan.

"Aye, but they have snorted all the coke and now fucked off. Who is paying that, eh? You even have enough for that?", moaned Jack.

"Fuck you talking about? Do I have enough? You're only raging because none of them went with you", replied Allan.

Davey started laughing and Jack saw red.

"Fuck you, because you're shagging some skank", said Jack, gesturing towards Allan's girlfriend who was passed out on the sofa.

"Fuck you talking to? Apologize now", Allan said, rising to his feet.

Jack stood up to meet him. "You standing up to? Better sit the fuck down, standing up to me."

"You're out of order. Get the fuck out. Run back to Grease like a wee bitch", said Allan.

This was not the first time Allan accused Jack of being Grease's "bitch". It angered Jack more this time because just a few days prior, in front of Allan and Robert, Grease had reached out and clasped his hands over Jack's mouth to stop him complaining about having to "tap £40" to Grease despite having money in his pocket. This "disrespect" was enough for Jack to ask Mary and the children to move out. Mary was already aware of the growing tension between Jack and Grease, and was stepping up her search for homes in the area, even bidding on a house for let.

Jack punched Allan in the mouth. Intoxicated, Allan stumbled backward and fell through a small wooden sit table with a lamp on it, breaking the lamp in the process.

"Fuck you doing mate?", Davey chimed in. He stood up to help Allan, who looked dazed and confused.

"What you got to say about it?", barked Jack, grabbing Davey by the side of the neck and pushing him to the floor.

"You better get that bill paid, Allan", Jack warned on his way out.

Outside, Jack started to regret what he had done. Allan and Davey did not deserve that, but he knew better than to go back and apologize when things were still raw – that would only make things worse. Jack was too intoxicated to drive and too far from home to walk, so he did the only thing he could do – call Grease.

"Grease, it's Jack."

"Fuck you calling me at this time for? I'm in bed."

"Going to come and get me, please", Jack said getting straight to the point.

"Where are you? You crashed the car? What you do with the gear?", Jack could hear the fear in Grease's voice, the worry that the police were on their way.

"No, no. Fuck you mean, have we crashed? I am at Allan's. We had a fight. I punched him for being wide and slapped wee Davey too", Jack explained.

"Davey, fuck you mean Davey? Allan? What you doing punching him? Allan and Davey aren't supposed to meet, remember. Now you're hanging about with them, like?" Grease was angry. "Make your own way home. I'll see when I see you", he added.

Jack walked home.

Jack eventually got home at 5 am and was in the kitchen that afternoon, nursing a hangover, when he heard Grease enter through the front door. Jack heard other voices with him. "Fuck, it was Allan", he thought – and Davey as well.

"Jack, moan in the living room, eh", Grease shouted. "We need to have a sit-down."

Jack stepped inside the room and immediately spotted the laceration across the back of Allan's head. "No marks on the face though. Must not have been that great a punch after all", he thought to himself.

"Sorry mate, I was–", Jack began.

"Fuck up mate", Grease said, cutting him off mid-sentence. "Sit the fuck down." Grease was in no mood for bullshit excuses.

"Right. I will start. You three had been warned not to be kicking about with one another. Nothing against you Davey, but I didn't want you all hanging about. Not because I am wanting to be a dick, but 'cause it is bad for business. What you want, eh? Pals or money? You want paid, yeah?", Grease said.

No one answered.

"Course you all do, so fucking get with it. I give the orders. See, if you don't like it, get to fuck. What you think, you're irreplaceable? The only cunt doing their job round here is wee Robert and fucking Stacy", Grease continued.

"I am not saying anything Grease; I am just saying, we are all working hard as fuck. We needed a wee break", Allan tried to explain.

"Fuck you talking to? I know you need a break. But how did that go? You all end up battering each other", said Grease.

"Aye, but we do work hard. Just got out of hand, that's all", replied Allan.

"Are you saying I do fuck all or something?", Grease said, his face beginning to scowl.

"No mate, I'm not saying that", Allan said, backing down.

"If it wasn't for me, you lot would be fucking still doing fuck all", Grease added.

He had made his point. He then reiterated everybody's roles and responsibilities, and directed the trio to shake hands and make up. Allan and Jack had had many fights before, and just like then, they shook hands and went about their day as though nothing had ever happened.

By the next day, the boys had moved on and were back to business. That evening, Robert sold some Valium to one of Adam's friends in the park. Later on, Adam came knocking on Stacy's door, looking for Robert. Stacy let him in.

"Alright Adam", Robert greeted him as he walked in.

"Alight pal. I had to come to see you. See the Valium you sold that boy, the boy's dad is looking for who sold it to him. He had to go to hospital and get his stomach pumped."

"Fuck sake. Is he okay?", Robert asked.

"Yeah, but his family is raging. His dad is mental as well", Adam said.

"He know it was us?", asked Robert.

"No, but he will find out. His pals will stick us in."

"Fuck. I better call Grease", Robert said.

Grease was on the scene relatively quickly. He tried to reassure Robert and Adam that the situation was under control and that they were safe because he was there to protect them. The only problem was that Grease could not be there all day, every day. This is a common theme in the gangs literature – they always claim greater protection than they can actually provide because the routine activities of gang membership make violent victimization probabilistically more likely (see Decker et al, 2022). Predicably, it was when Grease was out shopping with Mary and the kids and not answering his phone a few days later that two older men in their mid-40s or early 50s showed up on Stacy's doorstep. Adam peered out of the bedroom window.

"Fuck mate, that's his dad", he whispered to Robert.

"Stacy, don't answer it", Robert instructed.

The knocking on the door continued and got louder.

"He's going to end up putting the door in."

"Alright, Stacy answer it and tell him it is only you that lives here", said Robert, fearful not only that the men might break the door down, but also that they were drawing unnecessary attention to the property.

Stacy answered the door while the boys hid in the kitchen and called Grease. They could hear raised voices coming from the hallway and Stacy tying to talk the men down.

"I don't even know what you are talking about", she said. "If you don't leave, I am going to phone the police."

"Okay then, call the police", the dad said.

This was the last thing Robert and Adam needed because if the police showed up, they would no doubt spot all the drugs and money lying around the house.

Robert rushed out into the hallway.

"Sir –", he said, as he approached the front door.

As soon as dad spotted Robert, he erupted.

"You wee prick. My fucking son is only 15 and you're selling him fake fucking Valium. He could have died", he yelled, pushing past Stacy and into the house.

Robert felt his adrenaline rising.

"Fuck off, get the fuck out the house", shouted Robert, as he now rushed to meet the man in the middle of the hallway. The two clashed, but Robert was immediately overpowered. The older man pushed him to the ground and punched him several times in the face. Robert felt his nose break immediately. He had broken it once before during a street fight with his female cousin of all people, so it was susceptible.

Adam emerged from the kitchen and tried pulling the man off of Robert, but to little avail. Adam was not a fighter, nor was Robert really. The man stood up, kicked Robert in the stomach one last time, then warned Adam to not show his face again in the area, as he knew he occasionally socialized with his son.

Grease arrived just as the men were pulling away in their car. Entering the property, he found Adam and Stacy taking care of

Robert, who was bleeding profusely. Grease tried to comfort them by saying the two men would be "shot", "buried" and "dealt with". However, as the days and weeks went by, nothing happened, and whenever Robert mentioned that day to Grease, his answer was always the same: "Don't worry, I am sorting it."

He never did.

Gradually, then suddenly

"How did you go bankrupt? ... Two ways. Gradually, then suddenly", Ernest Hemingway (1926: 136) famously wrote in *The Sun Also Rises*. In the case of Amy's gang in B-Town, the emphasis is on the *suddenly*. Objectively speaking, Amy's county line in B-Town was far more successful than Grease's county line in A-Town ever was. The operation went on for years with relatively few problems. However, that all changed one night when Gordon was arrested driving from Glasgow to B-Town in a car packed full of drugs. Police were on to Gordon after already dismantling one of gang's main suppliers in the Glasgow region, and it was the last straw for the organization's cocaine and heroin business. Police also cracked one of the gang's crypto networks used to advertise drugs and launder money, and a few months later, the cannabis factories operated by Amy's suppliers were destroyed in a revenge attack by a rival outfit. Just like that, as quickly as it all began, it was over. Amy still lives in B-Town and she still deals drugs with Echo and, to a lesser extent, Paul, though to nowhere near the scale that they used to.

For the boys in A-Town, the emphasis is on the *gradually*. After Robert was attacked in Stacy's home for selling fake Valium to a 15-year-old and Grease took no responsibility and no action, the group began to question Grease's authority. Grease and Mary had finally got a house of their own, a few streets over from Jack, so he was less visible now than he had been. Other than setting up the initial deals, it was felt that Grease now did little more than bully Jack and annoy everyone else. Grease was needlessly stockpiling drugs and routinely shorting the lads' wages, promising he would make it up to them next week, only to renege on his promise. Moreover, while he claimed to protect them, the assault on Robert proved otherwise. As Allan stated:

> 'You get fed up. [Grease] was there to organize everything. I was doing that now. He even had me starting to meet up with [Bob's delivery man] when he drove through. Fair enough, I wasn't bothered. He was there to be like the muscle. Robert had got heavily battered and he wasn't caring. The laddie's nose was broken. You just see things don't you. I owed £500 after that party. He took £700 to "teach me [a lesson]".'

Allan and others decided that they no longer wanted or needed Grease, and their growing resentment began to show in their actions. They stopped answering his calls immediately or sent 'dry' emotionless text messages back to him. They would knock off early on shifts. Grease suspected something was up, so he called for a meeting at Stacy's house.

"Look Grease it is not that we are saying anything bad. You see that Robert got battered and you didn't do anything", Jack said. Now Grease was no longer living with him, he felt empowered to speak his mind more.

"I said it would be sorted didn't I, but if I go round there and cause a rammy now, it will bring the police down on us", he replied.

"Some things are worth it. More to life than money", Jack pushed back.

"Jack. I have others to answer to. We start slowing down payments then we aren't going to get any more gear", Grease reasoned.

"So fuck. We can find someone else. Allan?", said Jack, looking over at Allan for support.

"Aye, well. You have Tam. He would sort us out", said Allan.

Tam was the best friend of the former drug dealer in the area, Chris. Chris had been the main mover of drugs in the region at wholesale level and above, with connections to organized crime in Glasgow, the West Coast and Edinburgh. He was a step above even Grease's gang back in Glasgow until he was incarcerated for drugs and firearms offences, alongside his brother and a few other criminals from around the country. Chris never sold directly to customers or even retail dealers in A-Town. Instead, he supplied his friend Tam, who, in turn, serviced the area from wholesale to street level. Tam was once the source for every independent dealer in the region, but with Chris no longer around, his business had shrunk dramatically. He was being kept afloat by contacts north of Aberdeenshire and in southern England.

Grease was aware of Tam and it was highly likely that Tam was now aware of Grease. Grease had himself considered trying to partner with Tam but decided against it because he was concerned that Tam would take over the line completely. After all, Tam was a local lad, one of the town's own. Grease always feared that the local community saw his line as 'an outsider thing' that they could never fully integrate and accept.

"Tam! Fuck off. He wouldn't supply you. We are already taking business from him. You think he is going to start supplying us so we can take more?", Grease replied.

"Why would he not? We would be getting it from him", said Allan.

"If Tam is having to go around buying drugs from loads of people up and down the country, he doesn't have that much. We have a steady supply. He can buy from us", replied Grease.

Allan, Jack and Robert wanted Grease to sever ties with Glasgow so that they no longer had control of the operation. With hindsight, it was a terrible plan, but they were desperate to wrest back control from Grease and they only knew half of his indiscretions.

Del hated the arduous drive up to A-Town. He preferred public transport, but there was no direct route from Glasgow to A-Town. It was arguably faster to travel south from Glasgow to

Newcastle, Liverpool or Manchester, even London, than it was to travel north into Aberdeenshire, the Highlands or Stornoway, and long journeys were not for him. Driving was easier, but the journey was full of windy country roads, hazardous turns and speeding boy racers overtaking each other on single carriageways.

Paddy would usually drive, and having someone else in the car helped Del pass the time quicker. This time, though, Del was traveling alone and at a time when he was supposed to be visiting his teenage son, who lived with his mother, Del's former partner. He heard his mobile phone in his pocket 'ping' a few times and knew that once he arrived in A-Town, he would find text messages waiting, giving him abuse and calling him all the names under the sun for neglecting his parental duties – again.

The last time, his phone actually rang; however, it was a call from Bob. "You fucking said give him a chance. You fucking said bring him on things. 'He won't fuck up', you said." Bob was livid. Grease had just reported several thousand pounds and an ounce of cocaine missing, presumably stolen. Bob half expected Grease had snorted the drugs himself and spent the money on parties and prostitutes, which is why he was 'summoning' Del to deal with it. In the end, Del had 'vouched' for Grease, so he was partially to blame in Bob's eyes (for a discussion of vouching in criminal networks, see Densley, 2012a).

This was the third time in as many weeks that Del had made this trip. The first time was because Allan had allegedly failed to pay his debts. Allan argued that Grease was, in fact, the one who dipping into his own supply and that was why the count was short. Del knew Allan was telling the truth, but he sided with Grease because Grease was his friend. "He is my boy. He says you owe it, then you owe it", Del told a rather shellshocked Allan. At least that was what he said in public. In private, he took Allan aside and slipped him several hundred pounds. "For the bill. I know Grease", Del said.

The second trip was after Robert told Paddy the story about selling Valium to some boy who had overdosed and then getting assaulted by the boy's father. Robert was hoping the gang might take revenge. However, when Paddy relayed this story back to Del, Del informed Paddy that the gang was not even supplying Grease with Valium. It was clear Grease was double-dealing and running his own side gig. Del, Paddy and Rav paid Grease a visit, but Grease denied the whole affair. Del punched Grease for lying, then forced him to take them to his local supplier, Jimmy, a friend of Tam's. Del warned this small-time addict-dealer that the next time he sold drugs to Grease, the gang would be back to burn his house to the ground and then "stab him to within an inch of his life". Grease then paid back several hundred pounds to Rav and Paddy for "putting up with his shit".

This third trip, however, was for an even more egregious offence – money and drugs had gone walkabout. This is a perennial threat in the illegal drugs trade because drugs are illegal, the drug economy is cash based and there is no legal recourse for drug sellers when transactions go awry (Jacobs, 2000; McLean and Densley, 2022). For obvious reasons, drug dealers cannot call the police or file an insurance claim if they are robbed, so it is the 'logic of violence' that regulates the market (Marsh, 2019). Del was the living embodiment of this logic.

When Del arrived in A-Town, Grease came outside to greet him.

"Alright mate, happening?"

"Fuck all mate. Bob called and said you have had some issues." Del cut to the chase.

"Aye mate. The boys have stolen gear. I think they took money as well."

"How you know it was them? You spoke to them?"

"Naw mate. I just know because Jack was in the house the other day. I was out round seeing wee Robert and his mate Adam. I come back and the money is gone", said Grease.

"What, you think Jack just took it? You lived in his house for months and he never touched it before." Del was suspicious.

"Anno mate, but the boys are trying to set up their own thing out here", said Grease. "Cut me and us out."

"What the fuck? You better be joking", reacted Del angrily. "You better be fucking joking."

"Naw mate. We had a sit-down the other night and they were saying about ditching us and doing their own thing", Grease disclosed.

"Take me to see them now."

"You want me to call them?", asked Grease.

"Naw mate. Take me to Allan's after we see Jack. Is he in?", asked Del.

"Should be at this time."

Del and Grease took the short walk over to Jack's house. Grease went to knock on the front door but Del stopped him. The door was unlocked so he just let himself in. Jack was sitting on the couch in his shorts and with a night robe on, feet up, watching TV. Del's big presence startled him.

"You gave me a fright there. Sorry, I didn't hear the door", said Jack. He stood up. "Want a coffee?"

"Sit down mate", Del said sternly.

Jack sat back down. Del came straight out and asked him if was plotting to cut ties with Glasgow and set up with another supplier in the area. Jack explained they only considered it because of all the problems they were having with Grease, giving Robert's broken nose as an example. Del told him the Valium issue was taken care of but the details were on a "need-to-know basis". He then made it clear that if he dared challenge Grease's authority again, especially in front of the others, he would be "stabbed in the face". To emphasize the point, Del spotted a plate lying on the ground with some food on it along with a fork. He picked up the fork in his right hand, grabbed Jack by the neck with his left and made to stab him in the eye. Del stopped before impact, then sat back down and moved on to the issue of the stolen money. Jack was shocked and surprised to hear that money had been taken, more so when he found out that it was over £2,500.

"Why would I steal it?", pleaded Jack. "I know Grease, I would be stealing from my own family, my sister. Grease, come on, you lived with me and I never took anything."

Grease chimed in, saying Jack had stolen the money to start up his own drugs operation. Jack was incredulous.

"What you think Del?", asked Jack. "See, if you think I took it, just batter me right now."

Del paused and looked Jack right in the eyes, as if he was trying to see into his soul.

"You know what. I believe you", Del concluded.

Grease was stunned and quickly fired off, ranting about loyalty. To Jack's surprise Del grabbed Grease and swept him off his feet and onto the sofa.

"Calm down, calm it", Del said. "I believe him, but he still owes the money, right?"

Now it was Jack's turn to be shocked. "What?"

"You were going to do the dirty on us. So, I would have usually done you in for that alone, but I didn't", Del explained.

"I would have preferred to get done in than pay all that", replied Jack.

"Well, I would have done you in and have robbed you of everything you own, so count yourself lucky. You did wrong, so you owe us £2,000. That is what was to come back. The other £500 is Grease's. That is on you mate. That is your fuck-up. Hide your shit better next time", Del said to Grease.

Grease remonstrated for a while, but the matter was closed. Neither party was happy, but at the same time, neither party wished to contend the issue too much. While £2,500 was a lot of money, in reality, they would pay it off in a matter of weeks, and in Jack's case, Grease already owed him about £2,000 in wages and tapped money, so they called it even.

Next, Del wanted to see Allan, but he did not want to leave Jack or Grease in case they forewarned him. Instead, he got Jack to text Allan and invite him over under the pretext of paying back the £50 he owed him.

Allan entered the property and walked into the living room, where he saw Grease before feeling Del's arm coming round his neck from behind him and grabbing him in a choke hold. He was forced to the sofa, after which Del patted him down with his free arm to check for a knife or weapon before letting him go.

"I need you to tell me the truth, Allan", Del said.

Jack signalled that the jig was up, and Allan came clean about the plans to cut ties with Grease. When asked about the missing drugs and money, Allan reasoned that because he was responsible for drop-off and pick-up, he would have already been caught if he was the culprit – either Robert would have noticed something missing on the front end or Jack would have noticed on the back end. With this, Del decided to call Robert and ask him what he did last night. Robert explained that Allan had delivered the supply. Adam and another youth then stopped by the house to 'get high' while he worked. Grease later came over to 'get high' with him, but also check the stock.

"Cheers wee man. Did Grease say to you about stock being short or anything?", Del inquired.

"No Del. He checked it. Sat for a bit and left", Robert said. Grease told Del he only said that so that Robert would not get suspicious, but Del was not convinced. As Del told us: "Obvious, either Grease was lying and took it to get Allan into trouble, or Allan had been cutting it short when he was dropping off. Why would he but? I was thinking Grease nicked it, took it to get Allan in shit for wanting to ditch us. Fuck knows really."

It seemed like Grease had taken the drugs and money mostly to get Allan and Jack in trouble with the gang back in Glasgow, thus reaffirming his position at the top of the group. It was an elaborate rouse that put Del in an awkward spot because he was friends with Grease and the one who convinced the gang to trust him in the first place. As Del stated: "I know it was shit, [but I] split it. 'Allan, you owe us half for the missing drugs; Grease you owe us half.' [In fact, I] took over half from Allan, two G[rand], same as Jack for talking shite about going elsewhere."

After this incident, it was agreed there would to be "no more happenings" because the infighting was becoming a major headache. In addition, Del discovered that the boys still had a kilo and a half of cocaine and several boxes of cannabis stockpiled. Payments had been short, and Grease and the boys had failed to deliver what they owed. Some months, they pulled in high sales; other months, they did not. However, the fluctuation had little to do with the market. Instead, Grease was simply ordering more than he could sell then adding to the bill every few weeks by withholding wages to the other boys. Del put a stop to that. He called Bob and told him to delay the next delivery to A-Town until the stockpile was sold and all debts had been paid in full.

Concluding remarks

In the organized crime literature, it is often said that what keeps criminals 'organized' and together in the absence of courts and contracts is bonds of trust (von Lampe, 2016). Trust reduces uncertainty regarding the behaviour of any partners in crime (Densley, 2012a). However, the literature also shows that people who tend towards criminality are rarely 'reliable, trustworthy, or cooperative' (Gottfredson and Hirschi, 1990: 213), and life in crime is fraught with uncertainty, distrust, suspicion, paranoid anxiety and misunderstanding (Gambetta, 1993). Betrayal is common in drug markets (Jacobs, 2000; McLean and Densley, 2022). This chapter highlights that trust in county lines is fragile, and in the end, violence or the threat of violence are often the only things keeping the gang together and the operation alive. Further, it highlights the fallacy of 'protection' in gangs and how gang membership really only elevates one's risk of violent victimization (Decker et al, 2022).

SIX

End of the Line

Introduction

In Chapter 5, we began to explore some of the issues that would affect the A-Town group's ability to sell drugs efficiently and efficiently, as well as erode their overall cohesion and credibility. As we will now see in this chapter, things only got worse. The tension between Grease and his employees in A-Town rises as their county line goes to war with another group in town. Accumulated debt, stock mismanagement, personal vendettas and ensuing violence cause the drugs gang back in Glasgow, who have their own problems to deal with, to lose faith and patience with Grease, and effectively sever his line. This chapter examines all of this, then looks at what happened next, whereby some local independent dealers are incarcerated and begin to desist from crime. This chapter concludes our case-study findings.

'The drugs don't work'

"Jimmy, mate, I am not saying that you're trying to bump me. That is not what I am saying", said Grease into his mobile phone. "Listen Jimmy, please listen", he pleaded.

Jimmy continued to scream and talk over him. "No Grease. You are phoning me up. Telling me I have sold you duds. Saying they are shit."

"Your pills are shit, mate", Grease came back. "You said it yourself."

Grease was angry now. Earlier that day, he had asked Davey to drive him around town running errands, none of which had anything to do with crime and county lines: a kid's bike he bought on Gumtree; a few bags of shopping ordered for 'click and collect' – that sort of thing. On the way home, though, Grease asked Davey to drive up to a house on the edge of town near North Village. The homes on this small estate were different from the cottage-style homes, flats and semi-detached and mid-terrace homes in A-Town. They were older, built for the traditional labourers of the town before the residential population grew, but nicely maintained, with manicured gardens and roughcast or pebbledash on the outside walls. All except one house, which stuck out like a sore thumb. This house was stained from the weather, with overgrown grass and weeds and rubbish bags littering the front garden, and in place of a curtain or blind in the front window was an old bedsheet.

"Wait here. I will just be a minute", Grease said to Davey.

A minute turned to 30. When Grease finally returned, he offered no apology or explanation; he just told Davey to drive him home. Davey did as he was told. He even helped Grease unload the car and put away the shopping when they got back. He waited for Grease to pay him for his time, and the patrol, but Grease never did.

Instead, Grease was waiting to feel the 'dunt' from the Valium he took at Jimmy's. Jimmy was the user-dealer who lived in the unkept house near North Village. He used and dealt heroin, mostly as a social supplier or low-level retail dealer, but he also sold prescribed drugs like Valium and non-prescribed homemade fake Valium on the side. Jimmy was Grease's source for fake Valium, which he sold on the side against the wishes of the gang back in Glasgow. Although he got caught, Grease was addicted – to the money and 'sneaky thrill' of running his secret side hustle (Katz, 1988), and to the Valium itself. He preferred the fake stuff because he had built up a tolerance for real Valium prescribed by doctors and medical practices up and down the country. Fake Valium was a bigger dose and a stronger high. Grease paid about £500 for each batch.

Grease did not know where Jimmy got his Valium from – Jimmy would never say. For a while, he thought Jimmy made them himself because he had made cannabis edibles and his own concoction of hallucinogenic 'drugs allsorts' in the past, but they never really caught on in the local community. At the same time, Jimmy was a problem heroin user, and his life was too chaotic to control all aspects of the drugs supply chain. Even if he owned his own pill press, he would have sold it by now for a tenner bag of brown in a dry spell. The drugs were obviously coming in from somewhere else. Not Glasgow, as Grease would have heard about it if they were. Little chance it was the Central Belt or West Coast either. It was likely somewhere further afield. Tam still made long-distance journeys to collect product. It was likely flowing in through him. Jimmy knew Tam, like most people in this small town did.

Grease still felt nothing. He took another fake Valium while putting the shopping away. He took a third before clearing out the hut in the garden to make space for the new bike, which would go in and never come out again, like the lawnmower and the kettlebells Grease bought earlier on Gumtree. After a fourth Valium and still no response, he decided to call Jimmy to complain.

"Jimmy mate, it's Grease. See them pills you gave me. They don't seem to be working."

"So? They have worked for everyone else", Jimmy replied, dismissive.

"Aye, but they are not working for me! I am going to need to get my money back. I will pay for what I have taken out of it already", Grease said.

"Can't Grease. That money has already been used. I had a tick bill to pay", said Jimmy.

Grease did not believe him. "Give me the fucking money back mate. How could you spend it that fast?", he said.

"My guy came round after you left. I had to pay him. Bring them back and I will give you the money back over the next few weeks", negotiated Jimmy.

Grease thought about the compromise for a second, but he knew that if he was in Jimmy's shoes, he would never pay his debt. Grease pushed back and Jimmy countered with an offer of £200 for the entire batch, which he would pay the next day. Faced with a loss of £300 and no supply to sell on, Grease blew up.

"Are you fucking mugging me off, ya prick? How long have I known you?"

"Don't get lippy with me, Grease. I will fucking stab fuck out of you", Jimmy came back.

This was a side of Jimmy Grease had not encountered before, though he was always wary of it. Jimmy was not the "type that would hunt you down", Grease said, but he had a reputation around A-Town for being a dangerous individual, somehow connected to other criminals in the region, including Tam, who was not inherently threatening, but could easily mobilize support from the local community, where he was well known and respected. It is not unheard of for local players like that to inform on other criminals to law enforcement agencies simply to eliminate them from the equation. Still, it is not in Grease's nature to back down. As Grease explained: "[I told him], see, when I see you, am fucking stabbing fuck out you. Selling me pure duds that you won't even get a small dunt off. I was raging. Heavy raging. Be fair, Jimmy is game. I will give the prick that."

Glasgow smile

Robert was genuinely enjoying life in A-Town. Despite leaving his family to move to an unknown world, spending several weeks sleeping on Jack's sofa, taking a beating from a fully grown man, enduring numerous threats from gangsters back in Glasgow and dealing with the "bitching and the fighting" from Grease, he had made real friends in A-Town. Allan, Jack, Davey and Robert were close. He was also making real money and helping his peers like Adam make it too. Robert had just bought a new car, though he had not passed his driver's test yet, so it was registered in Stacy's uncle's name. He was dressed in new designer clothes, living in a grown-up house and, best of all, sharing all this with the girl of his dreams, Stacy.

Robert was out that day shopping with Stacy. They had taken the day off together, and Adam and a new boy, Mark, were covering for them. Mark more or less worked for free, he was only 14 and enjoyed the name and reputation he gained among his peers for the activities he was involved in and the connections he was making. After shopping, Stacy and Robert took a walk in the park. They stopped to chat with a few local young people. Stacy was always popular due to her outgoing nature, and Robert was popular now too. He was far more confident, settled in a place where he felt he could be himself. Robert had a reputation on the streets for being tough but fair. The girls wanted him and the boys wanted to be him.

Robert noticed a tall, lean figure approaching in the distance. He was much older than everyone else and while he looked "dodgy", it was the middle of the afternoon and Robert felt safe in the company of his friends.

"Hi wee man, how is it going?", the man said, looking at Robert.

"Aye, good mate. You?", Robert replied.

"Yeah good. Is your name Robert yeah?", the dodgy man asked.

"Yeah, it is. Do I know you?", Robert asked. "Have we met?"

"Once. You're Grease's boy, eh", the man replied.

"No mate. I don't know what you're talking about", Robert replied, wary about how a guy he had never met before could immediately connect him to Grease. While the original cover story of 'Jamie from the East Coast' was long gone, only Robert's closet ties knew it was Grease who was pulling the strings in the background.

"I'm Jimmy", the man said. It was Grease's Valium dealer.

"Sound", Robert said, in an effort to deflect and ignore him.

Suddenly, Robert saw a flash of white in his peripheral vision followed by a blunt pain across his eye. Jimmy had punched him. While taller and older than Robert, Jimmy's punch was surprisingly weak. Robert retaliated, grabbing hold of Jimmy's tracksuit top, and a brief scuffle ensued until Robert felt a sharp pain running up his cheek, from his top lip to his right ear, followed by a dizzying warm sensation. Stacy screamed.

That was the moment Robert's stock bubble burst. His status gains were lost. No one wanted to be in his shoes now.

"He has fucking slashed you", one of the local youths in the crowd who was watching the fight shouted. "Oh mate –", another one chimed in, ashen-faced.

Robert immediately let Jimmy go and backed up. He put his hand to his face and felt the warmth of the blood spilling down his arm.

"What the fuck have you done?", Robert asked in disbelief.

However, Jimmy just kept coming. He lifted the knife up over his head and brought it back down on Robert. Robert raised his arm to block it, but felt the knife rip through his sleeve and cut into his arm.

Robert turned away and ran. Jimmy gave chase, but Robert was younger and fitter and was able to escape. Crouched behind a tree on the other side of the park, he called Stacy and told her to meet him back home.

Robert scared the life out of Adam and Mark when he walked in covered in blood and muck. He reassured them he was "fine", but once the adrenaline wore off and Stacy was dousing his face and arm with antiseptic, it was clear that he was in pain and pretty shook up. Robert picked up his mobile and phoned Grease.

"Grease mate, it's Robert. I've just been slashed across the face."

"Fuck sake mate. You okay?"

"I'm alright. It was some guy called Jimmy. I don't know if that is his real name. He said he knew you. A tall boy. Dark greasy hair pulled back. Think he was, or he has been, a junkie", Robert explained.

"I don't know who that is. Jimmy? Never heard of him. Probably a fake name", Grease replied, a little too quickly. Deep down Grease knew exactly who Jimmy was and why he was targeting Robert.

"What about the cuts?", said Grease, changing the conversation.

"The arm is bad. The face doesn't look that bad now it has been cleaned, but I am going to need stitches. Definitely in the arm", said Robert.

"Get yourself to the hospital. Get them to check stitch you. I will send Jack to take you. Don't tell them what happened but", Grease instructed.

"I think they will know mate", Robert replied sardonically.

"I mean it. Say you fell or got hit by a car or something."

Grease called Jack and directed him both to take Robert to hospital and to give him a "couple of hundred quid" to "keep his mouth shut" – knife attacks bring unwanted police attention. He then called Allan. As Grease recalled: "[I phoned Allan and] told him that prick Jimmy had just attacked wee Robert in the park for fuck all. What, just because I fall out with him, he goes and slashes Robert?" Allan was sceptical that this was really much ado about nothing. He asked Grease if this was a targeted attack, retribution for something he had done.

"Nah mate, nah, it would just have been by chance. Think he was walking through the park when heading to the town. He has probably just clocked. Aye, he knows Robert, he would know what he looks like. He has met him before with me. ... On the kit but, you know. He looks different, all gaunt and like shit", Grease deflected.

However, Grease wanted revenge and he was intent on "hurting Jimmy". As Grease stated: "Aye mate. I was on the warpath. The cunt comes after my boy and chanting he is going to do me in. I went after the prick."

Allan collected Grease and drove him over to Jimmy's. Grease got out of the car, marched up the garden path, picked up a brick and launched it through the front window. Grease then tried the door handle but it was locked so he booted it a few times. The door frame bent and the window panel cracked but Grease was unable to break in. He turned his attention instead to the bags of rubbish overflowing in the bins outside. He launched them at the property, scattering food and household waste across the front lawn. Grease then grabbed the makeshift curtain from behind the broken glass in the front window and pulled it down, ripping off the wall the curtain pole, which was only tacked on.

"Let's go. Before the police come", Allan shouted to Grease. Several locals were already peering out from behind their curtains, watching the action unfold. Grease climbed back in the car and the two of them sped off.

That night, Grease received three text messages from Jimmy on his personal mobile:

THINK YOU A GANSGTER [sic]
YOUR DEAD [sic]
DEADMAN

Grease did not reply.

Several days passed and nothing happened. No retaliation, not even another text message. Then, on a wet and windy afternoon, Jimmy and Grease met by chance outside the local supermarket in the town centre of A-Town. Jimmy perked up and stood a bit straighter and taller. Grease knew confrontation was inevitable, the only thing he did not know was whether Jimmy was carrying a knife again. Grease usually did, but he had left it back in the car, which was parked across the main road, so he retreated back in that direction. Jimmy sped up to cut him off, aware that either he was going for a weapon or was intending to drive off.

"What the fuck was that about at my house?", was Jimmy's opening gambit.

"You fucking slashed Robert. A wee guy. 'Cause what?", said Grease.

Jimmy told Grease Robert was "an accident" and that he was high when he attacked him. Grease was not buying it.

"We going to have a problem, or are you going to drop it?", said Grease.

"I don't have a problem. You started on me. 'My pills are shit. Give me my money.' Smashing up my house", Jimmy said, in a mocking tone.

Grease could see this was going nowhere. He reached into his car. As Grease told us:

> 'I offered him a square go, there. "You got a problem, let's sort it." He was pure, "I don't have a problem with you", [but he is] a sneaky cunt. I knew he wouldn't let it go. See him, see, if he had a dagger, he would have [stabbed] me. I was like, put my hand out [to shake his hand; instead], I pulled him in, malkied[1] him in the face, Junkie bastard. And [after he fell], I kicked fuck out him. Stomping his head into my car tyre. Prick.'

Grease viciously attacked Jimmy and only stopped when a local shopkeeper and another passer-by pulled him off. The police arrived at the scene and Grease was arrested.

Cutting ties and 'going solo'

News of these events eventually got back to Glasgow. Billy and Bob were angry at Grease, but Del was mostly just disappointed. He had kept the extent of Grease's double-dealing quiet from Billy and Bob, but Grease had now been arrested and charged for assaulting his Valium dealer in the street. It was clear that he had learned nothing. Del was also upset to hear that young Robert had now been assaulted twice and Grease had failed to inform him on both occasions. Grease's arrest and the assault on Robert were also so public that it was now widely known in the town that the gang was running a county line in the area, supplying one of their men, who was selling drugs and recruiting local youth. As Bob stated:

> 'I wasn't happy when I found out everything that was happening. Grease is a liability. He got charged for battering a mad junkie that had pulled a knife on Robert and stabbed him. He was selling drugs as part of his own thing. Bills weren't paid, and when they were, it was never on time and it was usually short. Grease saying he will catch up next time. I had enough of him.'

At the same time, the group was dealing with supply issues, financial problems and personal crises at home. Paddy, Rav and other members of the gang integral to its cannabis business had been charged with crimes and were either already in prison or facing a long stretch behind bars. The group's main cocaine supplier, a key member of another organized crime group, had also been sent to prison for attempted murder. The heat was on, not to mention that group members were cycling in and out of sex, drug and gambling addictions. Bob called a meeting and the group agreed to renegotiate the terms of their deal with Grease and the boys in A-Town. Bob called Grease.

"Got a wee proposal. How about you just run things up there. Without us. You have it sorted anyway. We will just send up what you need after your bills are cleared", proposed Bob.

"You cutting me off?", asked Grease.

"No mate. Just things have been hectic here, and now you are getting charged. You owe a fair bit as well. I don't think we can send anything till it is paid", said Bob.

Grease had been getting a steady shipment each month and anything not sold was just added to the bill on tick. Cutting ties was a relief for both sides. Grease liked the idea of the gang having his back, and it helped him project a sense of power among his subordinates, but he was behind on payments and had grown tired of the related responsibilities of the county line. Not to mention, the reality of having to report back to Glasgow was emasculating and embarrassed him. If he wanted to "fuck up", he wanted to be able to "fuck up" without having to listen to others lecture him about it. Likewise, Bob never really wanted to run a county line with Grease in the first place. He only did it because Del proposed it, and now Del had lost confidence in Grease too.

However, there were still some outstanding issues. Bob needed to recoup any outstanding debts and Grease needed to find a new supplier. Grease agreed to pay in instalments, which was amenable to Bob, though he never completely cleared his debt because the gang eventually disbanded anyway. However, finding a new supplier was tricky.

Once the heat died down, for a few weeks, Grease pretended it was business as usual back in A-Town, but he eventually found himself running low on stock and had to come clean with Jack, Allan and Robert that they had been cut off. The only way Grease could get drugs from Glasgow now was if the group paid in full in advance – no more 'tick' or credit line. Tam was their best bet for a new supplier, but because Grease had assaulted Jimmy and Jimmy was friends with Tam, he was reluctant to explore that option. It was at that point that Robert spoke out:

> '[I wanted] out. I'd had enough. Thought I would do it for a wee bit and get some money. I have a cut on my face to show for it. Having to live with it. I said, "I'm out." [Stacy's uncle] offered me a legit job. We had some cash set aside. If I gave it to Grease [to resupply on drugs elsewhere], we would never get it back. "I am out", I said.'

Robert said out loud what Jack and Allan had been thinking inside their heads. Grease was asking them to front their own money for a large buy to start again from scratch, but given past precedent, they knew Grease would never pay them back in full or on time. If Robert was out, then Stacy was out too, and that meant they needed a new base of operations as well. Adam and Mark would follow. This was everyone's opportunity to cut loose from the debts they had accumulated and to cut ties with Grease. Lest they forget, Grease had likely concocted the story about Jack stealing money and Allan stealing drugs. Grease's side business was what got Robert assaulted not once, but twice, and now the young lad was scarred for life. Robert complains about his arm causing him pain to this day.

The group disbanded. They said their goodbyes and everyone went their separate ways. True to his word, Robert quit the drugs game completely to work for Stacy's uncle. Robert and Stacy still live together, and at the time of writing, they are expecting their first child.

Grease surprisingly made amends with Jimmy. The two of them worked together for a while, selling heroin, prescribed pills and their favourite street Valium. Grease would do the drops and occasionally call on the services of Davey, who remained close with Grease and was happy to continue in the role of drugs courier. Grease was sofa surfing for a while but eventually moved back in with Mary and his children in A-Town. He continues to frequently float in and out of drug use, and distribution, with intermediate periods of legitimate employment. Grease recently became "bad" on street Valium and started dealing drugs again for a known individual in the Central Belt. He was caught by police with a thousand pounds in cash and several thousands of pounds worth of drugs about his person. He is awaiting sentencing.

Allan seized the opportunity to start his own drug-dealing operation. He met with Tam through a mutual friend, then had Davey courier him around the region while he dropped off Tam's drugs. The main issue Allan faced 'going solo' (Windle and Briggs, 2015a) was that he assumed more risk and responsibility, and because he was doing all the drops and deliveries himself, he was limited in what he could sell. He basically became an independent retail-level drug dealer, selling everything but heroin, and profits were minimal. Allan was eventually arrested for his part in drug supply in the area, and after a brief stint on the run and hiding out with the old gang back in Glasgow, he wound up in prison.

Jack occasionally sells cannabis as a social supplier to pay bills and fund his lifestyle but has otherwise drifted away from drug supply altogether. He still lives in A-Town, in the house Grease and Mary once shared with him.

Concluding remarks

This chapter has shown how county lines fall apart because of both outside influence and internal pressures. It confirms that the mythologized riches of county lines are precisely that. However, in contrast to the 'standard story' of county lines, it has also shown that drugs gangs in hub cities are often quite content to cut ties with the line because although it makes a profit, the '10,000-mile screwdriver' by which distant commanders use long-haul communications to micromanage subordinates comes with several headaches and heartaches. In the end, labour issues, supply and logistics issues, debt issues, fear of police and rival predation, and Robert's assault and permanent disfigurement all caught up with Grease and were enough for the gang back in Glasgow to call it quits. Less than a year after the county line in A-Town was established, it was dissolved. Some of its members went solo, becoming independent drug dealers, while others left the life of crime completely.

SEVEN

County Lines in a Therapy Culture: A Conclusion

Introduction

> A common feature in county lines drug supply is the exploitation of young and vulnerable people. The dealers will frequently target children and adults – often with mental health or addiction problems – to act as drug runners or move cash so they can stay under the radar of law enforcement. (NCA, no date)

> From the standpoint of a sociological analysis, the diagnosis of a growing variety of psychological harms today should be interpreted as an act of social construction rather than the discovery of objective facts. (Furedi, 2016: 34)

There is now a consensus among policy makers, scholars and law-and-order agencies – a standard story – that county lines pose a fundamental challenge to how drug markets and criminal gangs have been understood and policed in the UK (HMG, 2018; NCA, 2015, 2017, 2019). There are two principal challenges noted by the standard story.

The first suggests that county lines represent a significant shift in the organizational and economic rationale of how drug markets operate (Harding, 2020; Whittaker et al, 2020b). Changes in relations of supply and demand at local levels reflect changes in global consumer capitalism. In this sense, then, county lines embody a marked shift away from traditional localized markets and towards evolving, more globally informed post-industrial consumer-oriented models (McLean et al, 2020). The second key challenge relates to the identification and subsequent centring of the concept of 'vulnerability' within discussions regarding approaches to policing and prosecuting county lines networks (Moyle, 2019).

Both these challenges, the standard story suggests, undermine current practice and thinking regarding the policing of illicit drug markets. Traditional approaches to policing, predicated upon a normative understanding of deviance, criminal behaviour and the victim/perpetrator binary, for example, are no longer fit for purpose and require fundamental change. This is both a cause and a consequence of the standard story, and we readily admit that some of our prior research contributed to it (Robinson et al, 2019; McLean et al, 2020).

Our two ethnographic case studies of county lines in action do not demonstrate that the standard story is wrong per se, but rather, and consistent with studies that embrace their complexity (for example, Harding, 2020), demonstrate that county lines cannot be reduced to one narrative and one narrative only. Our findings contest the standard story in the following ways:

- People migrate from 'hub' cities to 'county' sites not just at the direction of gang leaders, but for personal, family reasons. Like Maxson (1998) discovered in the US, crime opportunities and drug market expansion may be secondary motivations for gang proliferation and gang member migration.
- Relatedly, it is people who have some existing ties to the 'county' areas, even local relationships within them, who are chiefly responsible for the logistics on the ground. These people tend to be adults, not children, because children are developmentally too young and too conspicuous to engage in organized criminal activity.
- While some drug dealers enthusiastically embrace the always-on culture of modern drug dealing and the use

of smartphones and social media to reach customers, others find delivery dealing a chore – and a risk – and they only do it to keep up with consumer demands and customer preferences. This suggests that the standard story that technology exclusively drives social change in drug markets and that mobile phones make drug dealing easier is a reductionism.
- Big-city gangs do not always supplant or subsume local parochial drug dealers; rather, they sometimes have to learn to live with them. County lines drugs networks may be regulated by violence, but too much violence is bad for business, and if events away in the county sites threaten the gang at home in the hub, the gang will cut ties in the interests of self-preservation.
- While the standard story emphasizes *child* criminal *exploitation*, the two youngest people in our study were 16 – old enough to leave school – and everybody else was an adult. Likewise, while some interviewees were demonstrably vulnerable and exploited (for example, Peter, who had a substance use disorder and whose house was cuckooed), many others were habitual offenders who entered into county lines of their own volition, fully embracing a life of deviant entrepreneurship. This includes women, who traditionally are portrayed as 'ideal victims' (Christie, 1986) in county lines, not agentic active offenders in positions of authority and leadership.

This final chapter discusses the broad implications of this latter point specifically. Here, we locate the standard story – with its particular focus upon the advocation of a more therapeutically informed approach to policing the issue of vulnerability within these narratives – within the broader sociological concerns regarding the historical tendency towards the medicalization of social issues and the co-option of psychological concepts, such as 'vulnerability', into non-clinical contexts like criminal justice and policing. Our goal is to highlight the dangers of assuming that you 'know it when you see it' when it comes to county lines and to encourage scholars to continue to conduct the type of grounded, narrative criminology displayed here, which can document diverse forms of this emerging and elusive phenomenon.

County lines and the pathologization of the everyday

Ideas of vulnerability and vulnerable populations have become integral to how criminologists, policy makers and law enforcement practitioners now understand illicit drugs markets and identify them as county lines (Spicer, 2019). However, the commuting drug dealer is not altogether a new phenomenon. Travelling from urban centres to the provincial hinterlands to sell has been a long-term feature of drug markets (Windle and Briggs, 2015b) and, as noted, a necessary feature of Scotland's illicit drug market (Densley et al, 2018). Nevertheless, rapid globalization, technological change, marketization and the post-industrialized consumer economy have given rise to the establishment of new, complex networks of illicit drug trade, transforming previously localized and largely unorganized activities into an organized, systemic and 'significant national threat' (NCA, 2019; see also Harding, 2020: 13).

Similarly, although vulnerable groups have always played a role in drug markets, which have 'long been characterised by unequal or exploitative relationships' (Moyle, 2019: 741), what is significant in terms of policy-informed definitions of the county lines model is the focus given to a deliberate and '*systematic* targeting and harnessing of vulnerable populations' (Windle et al, 2020: 67, emphasis in original) when establishing markets in new 'host' towns. Not only has vulnerability become a central feature in official policy discussion on county lines, but it has significantly recast how the problem of illicit drugs should be policed, drawing attention to wider weakness within law enforcement and the criminal justice system in the UK, as well as 'the limitations of traditional police thinking and practice' (Coliandris, 2015: 25).

Indeed, one cannot help but feel that the policing of so-called 'vulnerable populations' has attained far greater priority within law enforcement policy than either the dealing or consumption of controlled substances themselves. This is reflected in the use of non-drug-related legislation in the prosecution of county lines-type offences. In 2017, for example, the Crown Prosecution Service (2017) defined county lines as a form of human trafficking; as such, drug dealing could now be prosecuted under the Modern Slavery Act 2015. Youth once uniformly criminalized as 'drug dealers' with only themselves to blame were suddenly determined to have been shaped by forces beyond their control. In 2018, the first successful county lines convictions were made when the 2015 Act was used to prosecute dealers for child-trafficking violations (Windle et al, 2020).

The increasing focus on the use and exploitation of children and vulnerable young people in drug gangs has raised questions about how – if at all – the police should approach the issue. Police briefings and policy guidance suggest that descriptive terms like 'drug running' are no longer permissible and they should be replaced by the term 'child criminal exploitation', which allegedly captures the complexity of contemporary drug dealing networks and the nuanced ways in which adults target and coerce vulnerable populations and young people (Windle et al, 2020).

The adoption of a more therapeutically informed approach to policing drug-related crime reflects broader trends in law enforcement at both national and international levels (Nolan, 1998; Fitzpatrick, 2001). This tendency was first identified by sociological perspectives that emerged in the late 1960s and 1970s that began to critically analyse the extension of medicalized forms of knowledge and expertise into non-medical aspects of everyday life (Conrad, 1992, 2005, 2007). Sociology began to adopt a critical stance towards the array of non-medical phenomena and behaviours that were now becoming subject to the authority of the medical expert. Crucially, critical approaches to this societal expansion of the 'medical gaze' theorized it as a form of social control (Parsons, 1951) and surveillance (Foucault, 1965).

Early critics of the medicalization of social life not only pointed to the expansive character of the purview of the medical professional, but also outlined how this tendency involved a substantive recasting of how institutional authority would mediate its relationship with wider society. Irving Zola (1972) noted that the medicalization of everyday life legitimated the normalization of 'patient' status as the dominant expression of the relationship between institutional power and individuals in society.

The contemporary drive to medicalization, Furedi (2008) suggests, has two features that distinguish it from earlier forms. First, it is underpinned by the emergence of a much more culturally pervasive therapeutic sensibility and a much more psychologized character, whereby diagnosed emotional or psychological problems become the principal vocabulary through which contemporary social experience is understood. The second distinctive feature that Furedi (2008: 108) suggests is that the contemporary medicalization of social life is no longer regarded as a negative phenomenon and, as we shall see later, is largely encouraged as a progressive feature for dealing with social problems in a more empathetic and compassionate way. Therapeutic language now plays a major role in the way individuals now make sense of their lives and construct identities for themselves, and how these identities are reflected in and through new forms of moral and social authority.

Haslam (2016) points to a process that he identifies as 'concept creep'. This is a social process whereby formerly clinically bound psychological concepts become much more culturally pervasive and begin to confer meaning on a range of behaviours and social phenomena traditionally outside the diagnostic purview of psychology (Haslam, 2016; Haslam and McGrath, 2020). Via concept creep, psychological terms of reference and diagnostic concepts undergo significant 'semantic change', cultural expansion and redefinition. Haslam (2016: 2) argues that this process has been systematic in the way that it has 'targeted a particular type of concept'. In particular, he suggests, it 'targets' those concepts that have specific negative salience and accentuate pathological or undesirable aspects of human experience and behaviour. Haslam and McGrath (2020: 514) argue that the 'proposition that harm is the thematic drawstring' that shapes the expansion of psychologized frameworks of understanding is central to comprehending this process.

Within this process, moreover, the conceptual meaning loses its clinical specificity and is expanded to apply to an 'enlarged range of additional phenomena' (Haslam, 2016: 2). Via concept creep, clinical or diagnostic definitions become much broader and subjective in application and interpretation. Furedi (2008) calls this process 'diagnosis expansion' and emphasizes the de-professionalized character of the process, wherein non-medical forms of authority and expertise utilize therapeutic/medicalized concepts as a form of explanation. Furedi (2008: 34) adds that the culturally expansive tendency of psychology to inflate harms and 'expand the boundaries of trauma' is a 'powerful dynamic towards a reconstitution of personhood' and 'exemplifies the cultural salience of concept creep'.

The findings presented in this book question why therapeutic concept creep has become a central characteristic of the narratives on UK county lines and drug crime. A salient aspect of this 'diagnostic expansion', or 'concept creep', that is borne out by county lines discussions is that vulnerability has been normalized as a defining feature of the human condition (Haslam, 2016: 34). Policy and aspects of county lines scholarship appropriate increasingly therapeutic frameworks of understanding that problematize and redefine orthodox liberal conceptualizations of personhood, autonomy and agency. The co-option of psychologized frames of reference within criminal justice approaches to drug crime serves to negate the subjective basis upon which individuals ascribe meaning to their actions as autonomous actors. This apparent valorization of psychologized forms of understanding within approaches to county lines reconstitutes the norms, values and competencies of the legal and criminal justice systems that are charged with dealing with the issue.

Therapeutic jurisprudence's problem with binary norms

Nolan (1998) has drawn attention to how a therapeutic sensibility now largely shapes how the criminal justice system understands and deals with drug-related crime in the US. This has had the effect of undermining traditional approaches to law, order and criminality, which are now supplanted by an increasingly psychological nomenclature, wherein behaviour once commonly understood as crimes or legal infractions are recast as pathologies or forms of psychic harm.

Drug crime has shifted from a traditional correctional context into a predominantly clinical setting. As the distinctions between criminal and therapeutic become increasingly blurred and 'less clearly delineated' (Nolan, 1998: 83), the authority of a more traditional and binary-informed approach to criminal justice begins to be questioned. Indeed, the contemporary moment is characterized by more broadly problematizing the binary nature of moral and social life. Furedi (2021) has pointed to a tendency within academic and policy scholarship that seeks to negate, or, at best, renegotiate, the binary character of social life and highlights the dangers of binary thinking.

Recent criminological scholarship on illicit drug markets and county lines in the UK echoes this anti-binary trend, questioning the integrity of the prevailing value systems that inform policing and policy strategies (Coliandris, 2015; Moyle, 2019). Although the recentring of official approaches to gang activity around vulnerability and youth has, in part, been welcomed as 'progressive thinking' (Coliandris, 2015: 27), it is also noted that there is a lack of clarity within official definitions of vulnerability. According to Moyle (2019: 742), the absence of a 'definitive categorization of groups that should be considered as vulnerable' within UK law severely compromises the ability of the criminal justice system and police to respond in effective and legitimate ways, especially as 'the county lines model presents a complex situation in which participating labourers might not necessarily meet the parameters of "traditional" notions of vulnerability'. This sentiment is echoed elsewhere, particularly about criminal justice and policing practices that do not, or rather cannot, recognize 'the precise contours and factors underpinning vulnerability' (Coliandris, 2015: 27).

Current scholarship on county lines suggests that the binary thinking that informs police practice – predicated upon 'idealized' understandings of vulnerability and normative notions of victimhood – hinders the safeguarding of those exploited by county lines gangs and exacerbates the vulnerability of those it purports to be trying to help (Windle et al, 2020). Following Coliandris (2015), Moyle (2019) draws attention to the tendency within normative policing of drug-related crime to recycle notions of idealized binary counter positions that falsely delineate criminal activity and victimhood. A key feature of this argument is the proposition that the binary distinction between victim and perpetrator that shapes current legal and criminal justice practice is no longer tenable.

Scholars suggest that the binary thinking engrained in criminal justice systems unwittingly misinterprets involvement in deviant or risky activity, such as drug dealing, as an expression of rational choice on the part of the participant. This, they suggest, creates institutional knowledge that reproduces the conceptual hierarchies through which the status of vulnerability is conferred. Munro and Scoular (2012) have referred to this as a 'politics of vulnerability', which defines who and 'who is not recognised to be vulnerable, and in what conditions' (Moyle, 2019: 742). Rarely are marginalized youth seen as 'victims' of public policy or structural inequality, for instance.

The politics of vulnerability: county lines and concept creep

The tendency towards medicalization has attained a very different significance within contemporary everyday life and experience. A notable expression of this is a shift in how forms of institutionalized knowledge, in particular, non-medical academic knowledge, adopt more accommodating positions to what has been previously considered a negative process. As Furedi (2008: 102) has noted: 'Since the 1980s, opposition to medicalisation has been minimal.' Perspectives that would have positioned themselves in opposition to the medicalization tendency in the past now appear to see it as a potentially liberating, empowering and compassionately progressive development.

This new contextual environment has meant that the medicalization process has lost its overtly medicalized character. The expansion and semantic change of medicalized terms intersects with a culturally permissive therapeutic discourse to inform new non-medicalized expressions of institutional authority. For example, in the case of the county lines discussion, non-medical experts now appropriate psychological concepts as they engage with the issue. Clinical terms are now often used by criminologists to describe drug-related policing (see, for example, Coliandris, 2015).

This apparent therapeutic turn in contemporary criminology accentuates the inadequacy of traditional criminal justice approaches and demands fundamental culture change within police practice. For Coliandris (2015: 34), county lines bring into sharp focus 'the interconnected-issues of vulnerability and safeguarding' as potential points of structural reorientation around 'questions about the proper roles and responsibilities of police services in democratic societies'. Coliandris (2015: 34) argues that the policing of vulnerability offers a 'promising framework for tackling not just the County Lines problems but a range of other sometimes overlapping challenges that see vulnerable people coming to occupy victim and perpetrator status – sometimes simultaneously'. Key to redefining policing culture 'will be a recognition by practitioners that vulnerability is a universal human trait and a process; as such, it is best understood by reference to the complex and dynamic interplay of personal, family, culture and social conditions' (Coliandris, 2015: 34).

While specific to a discussion on county lines, these trends suggest a marked push to reorient policing and criminal justice regimes onto a much more consciously therapeutic footing, as outlined by Nolan (1998). Moreover, the forefronting of vulnerability as a driver of institutional change suggests an expansion of the range and forms of behaviour and social activity previously considered well beyond the purview of policing systems as newly legitimate and necessary points of state intervention. This seems borne out by current government agency advice on how to identify county lines activity. On their website, the NCA (no date) provides a list of activities or behaviours that can be used by members of the public to understand 'if county lines drug dealing is happening in your area'. Things the NCA asks residents to watch out for include:

- an increase in visitors and cars to a house or flat;
- new faces appearing at the house or flat;
- new and regularly changing residents (for example, different accents compared to the local accent);
- change in residents' mood and/or demeanour (for example, secretive/withdrawn/aggressive/emotional);
- substance misuse and/or drug paraphernalia;
- changes in the way young people you might know dress;
- unexplained, sometimes unaffordable new things (for example, clothes, jewellery, cars, and so on);
- residents or young people you know going missing, maybe for long periods of time;
- young people seen in different cars/taxis driven by unknown adults;

- young people seeming unfamiliar with your community or where they are;
- truancy, exclusion, disengagement from school;
- an increase in anti-social behaviour in the community; and
- unexplained injuries.

If, however, one remains unsure that the brand-new top-of-the-range smartphone that the new next-door neighbour's surly, untalkative teenager has just acquired is proof that a county lines network is operating in the area, the NCA (no date) suggests: 'The best advice is to trust your instincts. Even if someone isn't involved in county lines drug dealing, they may be being exploited in some other way, so it's always worth speaking out.'

This broad 'exploitation' lens means that when police arrest young people in county lines, they often use as a diagnostic tool the National Referral Mechanism (NRM), a framework through which potential victims of trafficking in the UK are identified, so that they can be supported and protected. While this reduces criminalization, the problem is the NRM, a civil process, was never intended to be used on UK-born youth or in the context of county lines and it offers no guarantee of protection. The system is now overwhelmed with alleged child criminal exploitation cases and resulting delays in processing and decision-making leave 'victims' in limbo, 'vulnerable' to re-victimization ahead of criminal trials, especially if typical 'safeguarding' responses such as care placements amplify their risks and needs.

Further, the systematic incorporation of notions of vulnerability within institutional responses to the issue of illicit drugs provides the legitimation for the policing of an expansive range of behaviour within local communities. The co-option of this therapeutic, psychologized frame of reference within county lines narratives is consistent with the broader social and cultural process of medicalization and psychological concept creep that first began to emerge in Western societies in the mid-to-late 20th century. However, where once there was critical resistance to this process, contemporary criminology, as well as the social sciences more broadly, seem to be much more welcoming of these pathologizing tendencies.

Structural vulnerability and criminal autonomy

Following Haslam, Furedi (2016) has noted how notions of vulnerability have become normalized within contemporary accounts of human subjectivity and personhood. Significantly, this therapeutic turn is underpinned by the concept's use as a mode of identity management, rather than as a clinical technique or tool for the care of psychic disorder (Furedi, 2016; Pupavac, 2001). Predicated upon a 'radically pessimistic account of the workings of human subjectivity and personhood' (Furedi, 2016: 34), the contemporary valorization of vulnerability serves as the basis through which social power re-legitimates its relationship with wider society. Vulnerable subjects can only be protected and enabled by state and parastatal forms of therapeutic intervention. The institutionalized assumption of 'universal vulnerability' (Pupavac, 2001: 7) seems an apposite conceptualization of the outlook that has begun to shape policy and expert knowledge on county lines.

Coliandris (2015: 310) suggests that approaches to illicit drugs regulation need to reorient around the 'universal precaution principle', that is, an approach predicated upon the assumption that 'each individual is potentially vulnerable' and where policing strategies recognize vulnerability 'as the norm rather than the exception'. Indeed, in an echo of Nolan's (1998) argument that the therapeutic nature of US drug policy, in turn, reflects a wider attempt by the state to refashion and recast its relationship with US society, Coliandris (2015: 27) notes the 'symbolic importance' of the wholesale institutionalization of structural conceptualizations of vulnerability as a basis to re-legitimate contemporary policing.

As noted earlier, there is a claim that the systemic normative and binary thinking that informs orthodox policing practice towards county lines exacerbates a tendency towards idealized and privileged notions of vulnerability. These privileged positions *recreate* rather than *remedy* the problems posed by county lines. For example, as noted earlier, it is suggested that young people who are involved in county lines operations occupy a 'dual status' as both perpetrator and victim (Coliandris, 2015).

In light of this, Coliandris (2015: 27) suggests that the 'precise contours and factors underpinning vulnerability' need to be understood by agencies because a failure to do so will lead to further harm. For example, NCA (2019) guidance suggests that 'children who are not known to services and who have no previous convictions are also utilised in County Lines ... this means not being part of an organisationally recognised vulnerable group can mean that signs of exploitation can go undetected'. This view suggests that official binary conceptualizations of perpetrator and victim fail to recognize the complexity of the relations of risk, harm and exploitation that inform contemporary drug-dealing practice. This view explicitly identifies that the normative approach to vulnerability is a central weakness in combatting county lines, as well as policing and social welfare more widely.

In this context, the concept of 'structural vulnerability' has been suggested and encouraged as a means of reconceptualizing the role of the police and other agencies (Coliandris, 2015; Moyle, 2019). It is suggested that approaches framed through a 'structural' understanding of vulnerability, provide a basis upon which the systemically binary character of policing practice can be combated. Through reflection upon and recognition of the structural nature of privileged hierarchies of vulnerability, criminal justice institutions can identify often 'hidden' and unintentional biases that reinforce forms of exclusion and stigma.

Moreover, it is suggested that the normative institutionalization of an idealized conceptualization of vulnerability gives rise to a second problem: that so-called vulnerable populations involved in county lines or criminal activity more generally do not necessarily see themselves or identify as being vulnerable or at risk. While institutional responses to vulnerability, it is argued, 'often lead to the misdiagnosis or a failure of diagnosis', so too does the self-conception of the 'vulnerable' themselves (Coliandris, 2015: 31).

Coliandris (2015: 31) suggests that orthodox approaches to the labelling of particular behaviours or populations as 'vulnerable' are often 'rejected by the vulnerable person' as 'There may be stigmatising and disempowering consequences associated with being labelled "vulnerable"', which 'can adversely impact wider police-specific community relations as well as the individual's sense of identity, value and autonomy'. The point regarding autonomy is well made.

Moyle (2019: 750, emphasis in original) draws attention to the fact that 'contrary to police literature', research in this area suggests that 'there were as many cases where local drug users described a *willingness* to undertake this labour, despite numerous associated risks'. Moreover, this 'willingness' is seen as an integral aspect of the ways in which individuals negotiate their access to illicit drugs. As Moyle (2019: 750): 'For those in the midst of chaotic drug careers, without the resources to otherwise pay for their drug use, the county lines economy provided a "mutually beneficial" labour opportunity, albeit one that appears inherently exploitative for swift and reliable access to drugs'.

As Windle et al (2020: 71) suggest: 'While law enforcement narratives portray county lines as inherently exploitative, adult cuckooed residents reported to Moyle (2019) that they initially considered renting arrangements and drug running a "mutually beneficial relationship".' Moreover, Windle et al (2020: 71) continue that 'many vulnerable young people' interviewed in the research 'did not necessarily see themselves as victims'. This refusal is also reported in other findings. In research into young girls in secure units, Ellis (2018) notes that young people who are generally considered as vulnerable or at risk by institutional authorities tend to reject the label because it undermines the more positive and proactive perception they have of themselves.

The concept of 'structural vulnerability' – viewing those that participate as runners or dealers in county lines as belonging to 'structurally vulnerable' populations – renegotiates the relationship between criminal justice practice and the ideas of culpability, responsibility and agency that define liberal criminal justice systems. Structural vulnerability provides a rationale for more therapeutic forms of state intervention that move outside the traditional rights-based criminal justice framework. Core to this shift is an unquestioned (but nonetheless problematic) assertion that the 'victim' lacks the capacity to make decisions that are 'properly' their own or in their own interest. The normative 'misdiagnosis' that views participation in county lines markets as the result of choices made by individuals is supplanted by an approach that now begins with the premise that it is illegitimate of criminal justice systems to expect 'structurally vulnerable' populations to 'behave "responsibly" in the face of disadvantage' (Moyle, 2019: 751).

'Structural vulnerability' is a mechanism whereby the increasingly expansive, blurred and contested conceptualizations of vulnerability are normalized as the point around which policing structures begin to reorganize and reorient around the therapeutic as a new, almost non-legal point of intervention. 'Structural vulnerability' and the idea of 'structurally vulnerable' populations negates normative questions of agency, judgement and responsibility. They serve as a means by which law enforcement is re-legitimated as a therapeutic enterprise. The criminal justice approach to drug crime is subordinated to an institutionalized therapeutic world view and the culturally expansive pathologizing tendencies identified by concept creep (Haslam, 2016).

Concluding remarks

The two case studies in this book present a subtle challenge to the 'standard story' of county lines. The centring of vulnerability and the vulnerable within these county lines narratives suggests that the policing and enforcement of drug laws in the UK has undergone significant 'concept creep'. Sometimes, county lines are not county lines at all, but rather jargon for good old-fashioned drug selling. The idioms and nomenclature of county lines narratives are consistent with the medicalization of social experience and the tendency by institutional authority to understand social behaviour through an increasingly pathological lens. Labelling any and all drug sellers as exploiters of the vulnerable will invariably result in a more punitive response to drug harms, including harsher sentencing for petty drug dealers.

As Furedi (2016) notes, the concept of vulnerability has become so culturally engrained that it often goes without critical comment or questioning. Therefore, while Harding (2020) points to a reluctance among scholars to acknowledge the impact that county lines developments have had on exacerbating the tendency towards the formal organization and structuring of gang activity (see, for example, Whittaker et al, 2020b), there appears to be an increasing reluctance within policy and practice circles to critically engage with the marked psychologization of the conceptual framework that is now used to define county lines and related illicit drug-related behaviours. Apart from exaggerating an already problematic tendency towards the widening definition of socially problematic or criminal behaviour, the expansive and seemingly catch-all nature of the county lines 'vulnerability' narrative brings to the fore a general acceptance of the tendency to reduce what are in effect specific cultural and spatially nuanced activities to ill-defined, generalizable therapeutic categories.

The contemporary character of the pathologization of social agency through such concepts as 'structural vulnerability', in turn, gets justified as a more caring and non-judgemental approach to social problems. However, as Nolan (1998) suggests, therapeutic jurisprudence is often more punitive than traditional adjudicative approaches because the subject is locked into a much more intrusive and temporally indeterminate relationship with the state. Recipients of therapeutic justice are often 'subject to greater intrusiveness into their private lives than are other prisoners or criminal defendants, in that judges and councillors delve into personal matters once largely left outside the purview of the courts' (Nolan, 1998: 125).

Worse, social control, which has usually been managed by the state and state agencies, could be removed from government and placed in the hands of the private sector. The emergence of any new government policy priority – like county lines – is typically associated with new funding streams, but this too may contribute to slippage in the use of the term, inadvertently encouraging a 'social control entrepreneurship' that diverts people *into* systems rather than keeping people out of them as proposed (Warren, 1981; Cohen, 1985). The therapeutic character of county lines narratives suggests a fundamental reconstitution of the function and purpose of criminal justice and law enforcement in the UK. Attempts to normalize ideas of subjective vulnerability and the undermining of liberal juridical assumptions of individual agency seem to be readily accepted by policy makers and proponents of a therapeutically informed criminology. Might this not be the real source of the drug problem in the UK?

Notes

one County Lines and the 'Standard Story': An Introduction

[1] We have found that county lines practitioners often parrot the same talking points and use the same examples, presumably because they have all attended the same conferences and completed the same continuing education courses.

two Whose Line Is It Anyway?

[1] The 1961 United Nations Single Convention on Narcotic Drugs introduced four schedules of controlled drugs and was followed in the UK by the Misuse of Drugs Act 1971, with drugs categorized in Classes A, B or C according to perceived harm and therapeutic value. Class A is the category that attracts the most severe penalties for possession, supply and trafficking. The Misuse of Drugs Act, with amendments, is still the main law regulating drug use in Britain.

four Life on the Line

[1] Keyser Söze is a fictional character from the 1995 film, *The Usual Suspects*, constructed to hide the crimes of a criminal mastermind.

six End of the Line

[1] A slang term from Glasgow and West Scotland, used to describe slashing someone with an open razor.

References

Andell, J. and Pitts, J. (2018) The end of the line? The impact of county lines drug distribution on youth crime in a target destination. *Youth and Policy*. Available at: https://www.youthandpolicy.org/articles/the-end-of-the-line/

Andell, P. (2019) *Thinking Seriously about Gangs*. Cham: Palgrave Macmillan.

Black, C. (2020) *Independent Review of Drugs*. London: Home Office.

Bonning, J. and Cleaver, K. (2021) 'There is no war on drugs': an investigation into county line drug networks from the perspective of a London borough. *The Police Journal: Theory, Practice and Principles*, 94(4): 443–61.

Brewster, B., Robinson, G., Silverman, B.W. and Walsh, D. (2021) COVID-19 and child criminal exploitation in the UK: implications of the pandemic for county lines. *Trends in Organized Crime*. Available at: https://doi.org/10.1007/s12117-021-09442-x

Britt, T.W. and Dickinson, J.M. (2006) Morale during military operations: a positive psychology approach. In T.W. Britt, C.A. Castro and A.B. Adler (eds) *Military Life: The Psychology of Serving in Peace and Combat: Military Performance*. Westpoint, CT: Praeger Security International, pp 157–84.

Casey, J., Hay, G., Godfrey, C. and Parrot, S. (2009) *Assessing the Scale and Impact of Illicit Drug Markets in Scotland*. Edinburgh: Scottish Government.

Children's Society, The (2019) Counting lives: responding to children who are criminally exploited. Available at: www.childrenssociety.org.uk/sites/default/files/counting-lives-report.pdf

Christie, N. (1986) The ideal victim. In E. Fattah (ed) *From Crime Policy to Victim Policy*. London: Palgrave Macmillan, pp 17–30.

Clark, A., Fraser, A. and Hamilton-Smith, N. (2021) Networked territorialism: the routes and roots of organised crime. *Trends in Organized Crime*, 24: 246–62.

Clarke, R. (2012) Opportunity makes the thief. Really? And so what? *Crime Science*, 1: 3. Available at: https://doi.org/10.1186/2193-7680-1-3

Cloward, R. and Ohlin, L. (1960) *Delinquency and Opportunity*. New York: Free Press.

Cohen, S. (1985) *Visions of Social Control*. Bristol: Policy Press.

Coliandris, G. (2015) County lines and wicked problems: exploring the need for improved policing approaches to vulnerability and early intervention. *Australian Policing*, 7(2): 25–35.

Conrad, P. (1992) Medicalisation and social control. *Annual Review of Sociology*, 18: 209–32.

Conrad, P. (2005) The shifting engines of medicalisation. *Journal of Health and Social Behaviours*, 46(1): 3–14.

Conrad, P. (2007) *The Medicalisation of Society*. Baltimore, MD: Johns Hopkins University Press.

Coomber, R. (2006) *Pusher Myths*. London: Free Association Books.

Coomber, R. and Moyle, L. (2018) The changing shape of street-level heroin and crack supply in England: commuting, holidaying and cuckooing drug dealers across 'county lines'. *British Journal of Criminology*, 58: 1323–42.

Cornish, D. and Clarke, R. (1986) *The Reasoning Criminal*. New York: Springer.

Crown Prosecution Service (2017) *Human Trafficking, Smuggling and Slavery*. London: Author.

Daly, M. (2017) What happened to the 'Trainspotting' generation of heroin users? *Vice*. Available at: www.vice.com/en_us/article/8qqa94/this-is-what-happened-to-the-trainspotting-generation-of-heroin-users

Davies, A. (2013) *City of Gangs*. London: Hodder & Stoughton.

Decker, S., Pyrooz, D. and Densley, J. (2022) *On Gangs*. Philadelphia, PA: Temple University Press.

Densley, J. (2012a) Street gang recruitment: signaling, screening and selection. *Social Problems*, 59: 301–21.

Densley, J. (2012b) The organisation of London's street gangs. *Global Crime*, 13(1): 42–64.

Densley, J. (2013) *How Gangs Work*. New York: Palgrave Macmillan.

Densley, J. (2014) It's gang life, but not as we know it: the evolution of gang business. *Crime & Delinquency*, 60(4): 517–46.

Densley, J. and Stevens, A. (2015) 'We'll show you gang': the subterranean structuration of gang life in London. *Criminology & Criminal Justice*, 15(1): 102–20.

Densley, J., McLean, R., Deuchar, R. and Harding, S. (2018) An altered state? Emergent changes to illicit drug markets and distribution networks in Scotland. *International Journal of Drug Policy*, 58: 113–20.

Densley, J., McLean, R., Deuchar, R. and Harding, S. (2019) Progression from cafeteria to à la carte offending: Scottish organised crime narratives. *Howard Journal of Crime and Justice*, 58(2): 161–79.

Densley, J., Deuchar, R. and Harding, S. (2020) An introduction to gangs and serious youth violence in the United Kingdom. *Youth Justice*, 20(1–2): 3–10.

Deuchar, R. (2009) *Gangs, Marginalised Youth and Social Capital*. Stoke-On-Trent: Trentham.

Deuchar, R., McLean, R. and Holligan, C. (2021) *Gangs, Drugs, and Youth Adversity*. Bristol: Bristol University Press.

Doran, N. and Papadopoulos, A. (2019) Cannabis edibles: behaviours, attitudes, and reasons for use. *Environmental Health Review*, 62(2): 44–52.

Dorn, N., Murji, K. and South, N. (1992) *Traffickers: Drug Markets and Law Enforcement*. Oxfordshire: Routledge.

Doyle, P. (2018) How mobile phones changed drug dealing. *Vice*, 17 August. Available at: www.vice.com/en/article/ev889w/how-mobile-phones-changed-drug-dealing

Ellis, K. (2018) Contested vulnerability: a case study of girls in secure care. *Children and Youth Services Review*, 88: 156–63.

Felson, M. (2006) The street gang strategy. In M. Felson (ed) *Crime and Nature*. Thousand Oaks, CA: Sage, pp 305–24.

Fitzpatrick, M. (2001) *The Tyranny of Health*. Oxfordshire: Routledge.

Foucault, M. (1965) *Madness and Civilisation*. New York: Pantheon Books.

Fraser, A. (2015) *Urban Legends*. Oxford: Oxford University Press.

REFERENCES

Fraser, N., Hamilton-Smith, A., Clark, C., Atkinson, W., Graham, M. and McBride, M., with Doyle, M. and Hobbs, D. (2018) *Community Experiences of Organised Crime in Scotland*. Edinburgh: Scottish Government. Available at: www.gov.scot/publications/community-experiences-serious-organised-crime-scotland/pages/2/

Furedi, F. (2008) Medicalisation in a therapy culture. In D. Wainwright (ed) *A Sociology of Health*. Thousand Oaks, CA: Sage, pp 97–114.

Furedi, F. (2016) The cultural underpinning of concept creep. *Psychological Inquiry*, 27(1): 34–9.

Furedi, F. (2021) *Why Borders Matter*. Oxfordshire: Routledge.

Gambetta, D. (1993) *The Sicilian Mafia*. Cambridge, MA: Harvard University Press.

Geertz, C. (1973) Thick description: toward an interpretive theory of culture. In: C. Geertz (ed) *The Interpretation of Cultures: Selected Essays*. New York: Basic Books, pp 3–30.

Glasgow Indicators Project (2015) *Overview Poverty*. Glasgow: Glasgow Centre for Population Health.

Gottfredson, M. and Hirschi, T. (1990) *A General Theory of Crime*. Redwood City, CA: Stanford University Press.

Gunter, A. (2017) *Race, Gangs and Youth Violence*. Bristol: Policy Press.

Hales, G. and Hobbs, D. (2010) Drug markets in the community: a London borough case study. *Trends in Organised Crime*, 13(1): 13–30.

Hallsworth, S. and Young, T. (2008) Gang talk and gang talkers: a critique. *Crime, Media, Culture*, 4: 175–95.

Harding, S. (2020) *County Lines*. Bristol: Bristol University Press.

Haslam, N. (2016) Concept creep: psychology's expanding concepts of harm and pathology. *Psychological Inquiry*, 27(1): 1–17.

Haslam, N. and McGrath, M.J. (2020) The creeping concept of trauma. *Social Research*, 87(3): 509–31.

Havard, T., Densley, J., Whittaker, A. and Wills, J. (2021) Street gangs and coercive control: the gendered exploitation of young women and girls in county lines. *Criminology & Criminal Justice*. Available at: https://doi.org/10.1177/17488958211051513

Hemingway, E. (1926) *The Sun Also Rises*. New York: Scribner.

Hesketh, R. (2019) Joining gangs: living on the edge? *Journal of Criminological Research, Policy and Practice*, 5(4): 280–94.

Hesketh, R. and Robinson, G. (2019) Grafting: 'the boyz' just doing business? Deviant entrepreneurship in street gangs. *Safer Communities*, 18(2): 54–63.

HMG (Her Majesty's Government) (2018) Serious violence strategy. Available at: www.gov.uk/government/publications/serious-violence-strategy

Hobbs, D. (1998) Going down the glocal: the local context of organised crime. *Howard Journal*, 37: 407–22.

Holligan, C., McLean, R. and McHugh, R. (2020) Exploring county lines: criminal drug distribution practices in Scotland. *Youth Justice*, 20(1–2): 50–63.

Irwin-Rogers, K. (2019) Illicit drug markets, consumer capitalism and the rise of social media: a toxic trap for young people. *Critical Criminology*, 27(4): 591–610.

Jacobs, B. (2000) *Robbing Drug Dealers*. New York: Aldine de Gruyter.

Jaensch, J. and South, N. (2018) Drug gang activity and policing responses in an English seaside town: 'county lines', 'cuckooing' and community impacts. *Journal of Criminal Investigation and Criminology*, 69(4): 269–78.

Katz, J. (1988) *Seductions of Crime*. New York: Basic Books.

Levitt, S. and Venkatesh, S. (2000) An economic analysis of a drug-selling gang's finances. *Quarterly Journal of Economics*, 115(3): 755–89.

Marsh, B. (2019) *The Logic of Violence*. Oxfordshire: Routledge.

Matrix Knowledge Group (2007) *The Illicit Drug Trade in the United Kingdom*. London: Home Office.

Maxson, C.L. (1998) *Gang Members on the Move*. Washington, DC: US Department of Justice, Office of Juvenile Justice and Delinquency Prevention.

May, T. and Hough, M. (2004) Drug markets and distribution systems. *Addiction Research and Theory*, 12: 549–63.

McCarron, M. (2014) It is in the interests of justice and health to decriminalise drug users. *Scottish Justice Matters*, 2: 17–18.

REFERENCES

McCarthy, B. and Hagan, J. (1995) Getting into street crime: the structure and process of criminal embeddedness. *Social Science Research*, 24(1): 63–95.

McCarthy, B. and Hagan, J. (2001) When crime pays: capital, competence, and criminal success. *Social Forces*, 79(3): 1035–59.

McLean, R. (2019) *Gangs, Drugs, and (Dis)Organised Crime*. Bristol: Bristol University Press.

McLean, R. and Densley, J. (2020) *Scotland's Gang Members*. Cham: Palgrave Macmillan.

McLean, R. and Densley, J. (2022) *Robbery in the Illegal Drugs Trade*. Bristol: Bristol University Press.

McLean, R., Densley, J. and Deuchar, R. (2018) Situating gangs within Scotland's illegal drugs market(s). *Trends in Organized Crime*, 21(2): 147–71.

McLean, R., Deuchar, R., Harding, S. and Densley, J. (2019) Putting the 'street' in gang: place and space in the organization of Scotland's drug selling gangs. *British Journal of Criminology*, 59(2): 396–415.

McLean, R., Robinson, G. and Densley, J. (2020) *County Lines: Criminal Networks and Evolving Drug Markets in Britain*. Cham: Springer.

McPhee, I., Holligan, C., McLean, R. and Deuchar, R. (2019) Dr. Jekyll and Mr. Hyde: the strange case of the two selves of clandestine drug users. *Drugs and Alcohol Today*, 19(2): 133–46.

Moyle, L. (2019) Situating vulnerability and exploitation in street-level drug markets: cuckooing, commuting, and the 'county lines' drug supply model. *Journal of Drug Issues*, 49(4): 739–55.

Moyle, L., Childs, A., Coomber, R. and Barratt, M. (2019) #Drugsforsale: an exploration of the use of social media and encrypted messaging apps to supply and access drugs. *The International Journal of Drug Policy*, 63: 101–10.

Munro, V.E. and Scoular, J. (2012) Abusing vulnerability? Contemporary law and policy responses to sex work in the UK. *Feminist Legal Studies*, 20: 189–206.

NCA (National Crime Agency) (no date) What we do. Drug trafficking. County lines. Available at: www.nationalcrimeagency.gov.uk/what-we-do/crime-threats/drug-trafficking/county-lines

NCA (2015) *NCA Intelligence Assessment: County Lines, Gangs, and Safeguarding*. London: National Crime Agency.

NCA (2017) *NCA National Briefing Report: County Lines, Gang Violence. Exploitation and Drug Supply*. London: National Crime Agency.

NCA (2019) *National Intelligence Assessment. County Lines, Drug Supply, Vulnerability and Harm*. London: National Crime Agency.

Nixey, C. (2021) Drug-dealers are finding the always-on culture a chore. *The Economist*, 3 July. Available at: www.economist.com/britain/2021/07/01/drug-dealers-are-finding-the-always-on-culture-a-chore

Nolan, J.L. (1998) *The Therapeutic State*. New York: NYU Press.

Parsons, T. (1951) *The Social System*. New York: The Free Press.

Pearson, G., Hobbs, R., Jones, S., Tierney, J. and Ward, J. (2001) *Middle Market Drug Distribution. Home Office Research Study*. London: Home Office.

Pfaff, J. (2017) *Locked In*. New York: Basic Books.

Pitts, J. (2008) *Reluctant Gangsters*. Cullompton, Devon: Willan.

Presser, L. and Sandberg, S. (eds) (2015) *Narrative Criminology*. New York: NYU Press.

Pupavac, V. (2001) Therapeutic governance: psycho-social intervention and trauma risk management. *Disasters*, 25(4): 358–72.

Redthread (no date) A&E work. Available at: www.redthread.org.uk/what-we-do/#a&e

Robinson, G., McLean, R. and Densley, J. (2019) Working county lines: child criminal exploitation and illicit drug dealing in Glasgow and Merseyside. *International Journal of Offender Therapy and Comparative Criminology*, 63(5): 694–711.

Roks, R., Leukfeldt, E.R. and Densley, J. (2021) The hybridization of street offending in the Netherlands. *British Journal of Criminology*, 61(4): 926–45.

Roman, C.G., Decker, S.H. and Pyrooz, D.C. (2017) Leveraging the pushes and pulls of gang disengagement to improve gang intervention: findings from three multi-site studies and a review of relevant gang programs. *Journal of Crime and Justice*, 40(3): 316–36.

REFERENCES

Scottish Government (2020) *Scottish Index of Multiple Deprivation*. Available at: www.gov.scot/collections/scottish-index-of-multiple-deprivation-2020/

Secretary of State for the Home Department (2019) Independent review of the Modern Slavery Act 2015: final report. Available at: https://assets.publishing.service.gov.uk/government/uploads/system/uploads/attachment_data/file/803554/Independent_review_of_the_Modern_Slavery_Act_-_final_report__print_.pdf

Seddon, T. (2006) Drugs, crime and social exclusion: social context and social theory in British drugs–crime research. *British Journal of Criminology*, 46(4): 680–703.

Smithson, H., Ralphs, R. and Williams, P. (2012) Used and abused: the problematic usage of gang terminology in the UK and its implications for ethnic minority youth. *British Journal of Criminology*, 53(1): 113–28.

Søgaard, T.F., Kolind, T., Birk Haller, M. and Hunt, G. (2019) Ring and bring drug services: delivery dealing and the social life of a drug phone. *International Journal of Drug Policy*, 69: 8–15.

Spicer, J. (2019) 'That's their brand, their business': how police officers are interpreting county lines. *Policing and Society*, 29(8): 873–86.

Spicer, J. (2021a) Between gang talk and prohibition: the transfer of blame for county lines. *International Journal of Drug Policy*, 87: 102667.

Spicer, J. (2021b) *Policing County Lines*. Cham: Palgrave Macmillan.

Spicer, J. (2021c) The policing of cuckooing in 'county lines' drug dealing: an ethnographic study of an amplification spiral. *British Journal of Criminology*, 61(5): 1390–406.

Spicer, J., Moyle, L. and Coomber, R. (2020) The variable and evolving nature of 'cuckooing' as a form of criminal exploitation in street level drug markets. *Trends in Organized Crime*, 23: 301–23.

Stevens, A. (2011) *Drugs, Crime and Public Health*. Oxfordshire: Routledge.

Storrod, M.L. and Densley, J. (2017) 'Going viral' and 'going country': the expressive and instrumental activities of street gangs on social media. *Journal of Youth Studies*, 20(6): 677–96.

Sturrock, L. and Holmes, R. (2015) *Running the Risks: The Links between Gang Involvement and Young People Going Missing.* London: Catch22.

Von Lampe, K. (2016) *Organized Crime.* Thousand Oaks: Sage.

Walsh, D., McCartney, G., Collins, C., Taulbut, M. and Batty, G.D. (2017) History, politics and vulnerability: explaining excess mortality in Scotland and Glasgow. *Public Health*, 151: 1–12.

Warren, C. (1981) New forms of social control: the myth of deinstitutionalization. *American Behavioural Scientist*, 24(6): 724–40.

Whittaker, A., Densley, J. and Moser, K. (2020a) No two gangs are alike: the digital divide in street gangs' differential adaptations to social media. *Computers in Human Behavior*, 110: 106403.

Whittaker, A., Densley, J., Cheston, L., Tyrell, T., Higgins, M., Felix-Baptiste, C. and Havard, T. (2020b) Reluctant gangsters revisited: the evolution of gangs from postcodes to profits. *European Journal on Criminal Policy and Research*, 26(1): 1–22.

Williams, P. (2015) Criminalising the other: challenging the race–gang nexus. *Race and Class*, 56(3): 18–35.

Windle, J. and Briggs, D. (2015a) Going solo: the social organisation of drug dealing within a London street gang. *Journal of Youth Studies*, 18(9): 1170–85.

Windle, J. and Briggs, D. (2015b) It's like working away for two weeks: the harms associated with young drug dealers commuting from a saturated London drug market. *Crime Prevention and Community Safety*, 17(2): 105–19.

Windle, J., Moyle, L. and Comber, R. (2020) Vulnerable kids going country: children and young people's involvement in county lines drug dealing. *Youth Justice*, 20(1–2): 64–78.

Zola, I.K. (1972) Medicine as an institution of social control. *Sociological Review*, 20(4): 487–504.

Index

A

Aberdeenshire 10, 79
Adam 70, 76
addiction 13, 15, 88, 95, 99
  and revenue streams 39
advertising and logistics 69
agency 68, 105–6, 116
alcohol 9, 11, 71
Allan 14, 45, 51, 69, 79, 80, 84
  and advertising 66
  imprisonment of 97–8
  using the merchandise 71–4
'always-on' culture 57, 62–3, 100–1
amphetamines 13
Amy 16–17, 38, 46, 48, 49, 60, 61
  and 'always-on' culture 66
  and business 77
  and domestic violence 23–7, 29–32
Andell, P. 2
anti-social behaviour 110
A-Town 10–11, 13–14, 33
austerity 5
autonomy 68, 105–6, 113, 116

B

benefit claimants 65
benzodiazepines 10
bicycles 59, 68, 69
Billy 12, 13, 21, 22, 42, 94
  working with Grease 51–3
binary norms 106, 107, 111
Bob 11–12, 13, 21, 22, 42, 96
  opinion of Grease 51, 94–5
boxing 12
Brexit 5
B-Town 10–11, 16–17, 33, 50, 77
burnout 58
business, building the 34–7
  advertising 66
  'always-on' culture 57, 62–3, 100–1
  business back-up 43
  business management 32
  creating revenue 39
  keeping a low profile 43
  logistics and delivery 17, 61, 67, 69, 70
  management 69
  packing and pricing 55
  receiving orders 56
  recruitment 68
  roles and responsibilities 16
  stock issues 85, 86
  storage 44, 61
  stress 58
  supply issues 96
  workforce motivation 68

C

cannabis 56, 61, 71, 77, 98
  bagging up 55
  edibles 88
  growing 32, 51
  production 22
  'skimming off the top' 53
  wholesale supply of 13
care placements 110
Charles 29–30
children
  abusive childhood 15, 24
  child exploitation 1, 2, 4, 34, 67, 99, 101, 110
  limited use in organized crime 67, 100
  living in poverty 9–10
  and the 'standard story' 5, 20
  see also young people
Chris 79

cities as hubs 3, 4, 33
Claire 23–7
coal mining 11
coastal areas 3
cocaine 22, 32, 50, 55, 61, 71, 77
  wholesale supply of 13
coercion 5, 19
  coercive control of women 24
  into drug storage/selling 40
  of family 28
  and social media 31
Coliandris, G. 107, 108, 111, 112, 113
concept creep 19, 104–5, 108, 114–15
conflict 19, 50, 69, 92–3
  conflict with rivals 62, 86
  internal conflict 71–4, 78, 81, 82–5, 89
consumer demand 3, 54, 62–3, 99, 102
county lines
  business model 13
  defining 1–2, 18
  and 'intelligent design' 5
  'standard story' 4, 6, 19, 34, 67, 98, 99, 101
couriers/drivers 14, 46, 63, 97
criminal behaviour 3, 95, 100
  indicators of 109, 115
  and trust 85
criminal justice
  and definition of vulnerability 107
  and social control 116
  and structural vulnerability 114
  and the therapeutic approach 105–6
  traditional approaches 106, 108
criminology
  and clinical terms 108
  narrative criminology 7, 8, 102
  and therapeutic approaches 110
Crown Prosecution Service 103
'cuckooing' 4, 39, 49

D

data sources 8
Davey 14, 68, 69, 71–4, 87, 97
  delivery driving 64–5
debt 89, 96
  debt collection 19, 50
  increasing debts 60–1
Del 15, 79–81, 96
  disappointment in Grease 95
  and internal conflict 82–5
delivery dealing 19, 22, 50, 66, 101
Densley, J. 6, 55
deprivation 37
  and drug use 10
Deuchar, R. 48
deviant entrepreneurship 5, 48, 101
diagnosis 113
direct deliveries 69
disposable income 37, 65
domestic violence 16, 23–7, 31
double dealing 81
driving issues 80
drug dealing 31, 34–7, 50
  and access to drugs 45
  'always-on' culture 57, 62–3, 100–1
  bagging up 53, 55
  and child trafficking 103
  'cuckooing' 4, 39, 49
  and cybercriminals 5
  dealers as exploiters 115
  deliveries 69, 70
  delivery dealing 19, 22, 50, 66, 101
  double dealing 81
  drug runners 3, 6, 9, 99, 114
  edibles 55, 88
  equipment 41, 88
  poor quality merchandise 86
  pricing 9, 55
  setting up business 21–3
  'skimming off the top' 53
  supply issues 79
  urban 2
  and vulnerability 102–3

INDEX

'willingness' to participate 113
see also business, building the
drugs
  ageing population of users 10
  changing view of drug crimes 106
  distribution networks 7
  drug addiction 13, 15, 39, 88, 95, 99
  drug deaths 9, 10
  drug markets 6, 99–100
  drug supply 3, 12
  drug use and deprivation 10
  'glocal' drug economy 9
  transporting drugs 17
  withdrawal symptoms 10
  see also criminal justice; police and policing
Dundee 10

E

Echo 16, 24, 26–7, 32, 60, 77
  'cuckooing' 38–41
  rivalry 62
  and threats of violence 46–7
edibles 55, 88
Edinburgh 10
Emilia 61
employment 6
  drug dealing 5, 113
  lack of employment 11, 34
  view of legal work 37
England 4, 79
ethnographic fieldwork 7, 8
etizolam 10
exclusion, sociocultural 5
exploitation 19, 99, 102, 110, 112
  see also vulnerability

F

family 20, 28, 32, 34, 83, 100, 109
  exploitation of 41, 48
  lived experiences 37
females *see* women
fighting 12, 62, 71–4, 81, 90
  see also violence

Find My iPhone 31
firearms 3, 13, 15, 43, 60, 79
Furedi, F. 104, 105, 106, 108, 111, 115

G

gambling 15
gangs 2, 4, 50, 99, 115
  big city gangs 101
  'big gang theory' 43
  gang disintegration 95
  gang member migration 6, 20, 32, 33, 38, 100
  internal theft 53, 81
  joining gangs 5
  muscle 15, 45
  and protection 75, 78, 85
  racialized gangs 4
  rivalry 38, 62, 77, 86
  team work 22
  and trust 47
  and vulnerability 106
Gary 13
  unreliable nature of 22
girls, young 113
Glasgow 7, 8, 79, 88, 93–4
  and deprivation 9–10
Gordon 17, 46, 62
  arrested by police 77
Graham 36–7
Grease 13, 20–3, 33, 48, 69, 98
  after attack on Robert 92–4
  arrested by police 97
  attack on Jimmy 94
  authority questioned 77–8, 80, 84
  building the business 34–7, 41–5
  and deliveries 63–5
  drug selling 50–60
  and internal conflict 82–5
  managing conflict 73–5, 75–7
  mounting problems 86
  moving in with family 27–9
  supply cut off 95–6
  and workload 62–5

grief, dealing with 48

H

Harding, S. 115
harms 3, 105, 112
Haslam, N. 104–5, 111
heroin 32, 41, 57, 77, 88, 97
 and deprivation 10
 heroin addiction 17, 24
 and revenue streams 39
 users at the chemist 60
Hesketh, R. 5, 48
hierarchical control 47
Home Office Gang and Youth Violence 2
housing
 as business base 4, 28, 39, 44
 housing types 11
 and security 46

I

identity 111, 113
 and therapeutic language 104
individuals in society
 intrusion into lives 116
 as patients 104
industry, heavy 11
inequality 5, 9, 107
interviews 7, 8–9

J

Jack 14, 45, 48, 52, 98
 accused of theft 82–4
 and Grease 27–9, 41–3
 partying and fighting 71–4
Jacobellis v. Ohio 1
James 17, 60, 62
Jimmy 86, 92, 97
 attack by Grease 93–4
 attack on Robert 90
 and fake Valium 87–9
John 16
 imprisonment 60
 perpetrator of domestic violence 24–7, 29–32

K

knives and knife crime 3, 68, 90–1

L

lived experiences 7, 37
local dealers 3
London 4

M

marginalized youth 5, 47, 107
 and grief 48
marijuana industry 55
Mark 23–7, 24–7, 90
market analysis 6
Mary 13–14, 20, 28, 77, 97
Maxson, C.L. 6, 33, 100
McGrath 105
McLean, R. 55
medicalization of social issues 101, 102–4, 108, 110, 115
men 10, 19
Merseyside 5, 7
methadone 10, 60
methodology 8
migration of gang members 6, 20, 32, 33, 38, 100
mobile phones 50, 53, 66, 101
 burners 41
 importance of 5, 19, 57
 orders by 45
 and organized crime 2, 3
 surveillance of 35
modern slavery 4
 Modern Slavery Act 2015 103
money 31, 65, 70, 83
 arguments about 24
 easy money 34, 35–7
 mythologized riches 98
motivating the workforce 68
Moyle, L. 107, 113
Munro, V.E. 107

N

narratives 6, 18, 101, 105, 110, 113, 116

narrative criminology 7, 8, 102
National Crime Agency (NCA) 2, 109–10, 112
National Referral Mechanism (NRM) 110
night shift 69
Nolan, J.L. 106, 109, 111, 115

O

offenders' institute 12
organized crime groups 2, 10, 12
  and county lines 3
  low profile of 43

P

Paddy 15, 95
parties 71
Paul 17, 40, 46, 61, 77
peace deal 62
Peter 17–18, 38–40, 45–7, 49, 61
Pfaff, J. 1
pill press 88
Pitts, J. 2
police and policing 2, 77, 92, 94, 97
  anti-binary policies 106
  and drug markets 99–100
  policing and mythology 4
  policing of behaviours 110
  role of police 108–9, 111
  and structural vulnerability 114
  therapeutically informed policing 101, 109
  and violence 43, 62, 92, 101
  and vulnerability 102–3, 107–9
population 10
poverty 9
price of drugs 9
prison 13, 15, 17, 54, 60, 79, 86, 95, 98
'progressive thinking' 106, 108
protection 85, 111
psychiatric disorders 10
psychological concepts 101, 104–5

public policy and vulnerability *see* police
purity of drugs 9

R

racialized and marginalized youth 4, 5
Rav 15, 95
recruitment 68
Redthread 38
remote areas 3, 10
  'remote mothering' 57
revenge acts 62, 77, 92–3
risk 101, 107, 112
  risky behaviours 49
rivalry 38, 62, 86
  rival gangs 77
robbery 13
Robert 14, 44–5, 48, 52, 68
  attack by Jimmy 90–2
  attack by user's father 75–8
  and drug dealing work 58–9
  leaves drug gang 96–7
  recruited by Grease 34–7
  relationship with Stacy 69–71
Robinson, G. 48
Rudy 60
rural areas 2, 3, 10

S

safeguarding 108, 110, 111
Scholar 107
Scotland 7, 102
  deaths in 9
  Index of Multiple Deprivation 10
self-fulfilling prophecy 2
sentencing 115
sex work 61
'skimming off the top' 53
smartphones *see* mobile phones
Snapchat 5, 66, 69
social and economic harm 3
social control 116
social media 3, 5, 66, 101
  hacking 31

social problems 5
  view of 104
Stacy 14, 44, 69, 76, 90, 97
  and Grease 53–4
  and Robert 48, 70, 90
standard story 1, 2–3, 7, 57, 68, 100–1
state, the
  and society 111
  state intervention 109
  and vulnerable people 5
stockpiling 85
stress 58
surveillance 109, 110
Susanna 17–18, 45

T

takeaway drivers 14, 64
Tam 78–9, 88, 89, 96
taxpayers, cost to 3
technology 101
  see also mobile phones
theft 13, 15
therapeutic concept creep 105, 108, 114–15
  therapeutically informed policing 110
threats of violence *see* violence
trafficking 4, 103, 110
'Trainspotting' drug generation 10
truancy 110
trust 69, 85

U

unemployment 9, 14
United Kingdom, drug markets in 99–100
United States 1, 106
  drug policy 111
  and gangs 6, 33
'universal vulnerability'
  see vulnerability
University of the West of Scotland 9

V

Valium 10, 55, 57, 59, 71, 81, 87–8, 97
  boy hospitalised 75–6
victim/perpetrator distinctions 107, 109, 112
violence 3, 12, 19, 33, 46, 47, 49, 61
  attack by boy's father 75–6
  in the city 38
  Del's attack on Allan 84
  domestic violence 23–7, 29–30
  and heroin withdrawal 57
  James's attack on Rudy 60
  knife attack 90–1
  and police attention 43, 62, 92, 101
  with rival gangs 62
  and threats 81, 82–3, 85
vouching for others 80
vulnerability 1, 4, 47, 49, 99
  concept of 100, 102–3, 107, 115
  exploitation of 2
  'hidden vulnerability' 112
  and the human condition 105, 109, 111
  passive vulnerability 19
  and policing 101, 102–3, 108–9
  politics of 107–11
  rejection of vulnerable status 113
  structural vulnerability 111–14, 115

W

WhatsApp 5, 35, 66
wholesale and retail networks 3, 13
Windle, J. 113
withdrawal symptoms 10
women 19, 34, 101
  drug dealers 16
  female leadership 49
  sex work 61

work
  drug dealing 113
  illegal work 5, 48
  low-paid workforce 6
  workforce, happy 68
  see also money

Y

young people 47, 66, 99, 109
  racialized and marginalized 5
  recruitment of 6, 13
  young men 49
  see also children

Z

Zola, Irving 104